DEVELOPING INTERCULTURAL AWARENESS

A Cross-Cultural Training Handbook

Second Edition

L. Robert Kohls and John M. Knight

DEVELOPING INTERCULTURAL AWARENESS

A Cross-Cultural Training Handbook
Second Edition

L. Robert Kohls and John M. Knight

INTERCULTURAL PRESS, INC.

First published by Intercultural Press. For information, contact:

Intercultural Press, Inc.
PO Box 700
Yarmouth, Maine 04096 USA
001-207-846-5168
Fax: 001-207-846-5181
www.interculturalpress.com

Nicholas Brealey Publishing
36 John Street
London WC1N 2AT, UK
44-207-430-0224
Fax: 44-207-404-8311
www.nbrealey-books.com

© 1981, 1994 by L. Robert Kohls and John M. Knight

Book design and production by Patty J. Topel
Cover design by Patty J. Topel

Printed in the United States of America

05 04 03 02 01   6 7 8 9 10

Library of Congress Cataloging-in-Publication Data

Kohls, L. Robert.
  Developing intercultural awarenesss : a cross-cultural training handbook / L. Robert Kohls and John M. Knight.
      p.   cm.
  Includes bibliographical references (p. 137).
  ISBN 1-877864-13-7
  1. Multicultural education—United States—Handbooks, manuals, etc. I. Knight, John M. (John Mark), 1945- . II. Title.

LC1099.3.K64 1994
370.19'6'0973—dc20   94-1069
                                                          CIP

Table of Contents

Acknowledgments

Grateful acknowledgement is made to the authors and publishers who granted permission to reprint the following selections:

Batchelder, Donald. "The Martian Anthropology Exercise" from *Beyond Experience: The Experiential Approach to Cross-Cultural Education* 2d ed. (Yarmouth, ME: Intercultural Press, 1993.) Reprinted by permission of the author. Copyright 1977 by Donald Batchelder.

BNA Communications, Inc. For ideas on evaluation from the *Bulletin on Training*, March 1980. Adapted by permission of BNA Communication, Inc. Copyright 1980 by BNA Communication, Inc.

Casse, Pierre. "Communications and Intercultural Interactions." Adapted from *Training for the Cross-Cultural Mind* (Washington, DC: SIETAR International, 1980). Adapted by permission of the author. Copyright 1980 by Pierre Casse.

Damen, Louise. "The Form" from *Culture Learning: The Fifth Dimension in the Language Classroom.* Reprinted by permission of Addison-Wesley Longman Publishing, New York. Copyright 1987 by Addison-Wesley Longman.

Ferraro, Gary P. Six case studies from *The Cultural Dimension of International Business.* Reprinted by permission of Prentice-Hall, Englewood Cliffs, NJ. Copyright 1990 by Prentice-Hall, Englewood Cliffs.

Fieg, John P., and John G. Blair. For examples from *There Is a Difference: Seventeen Intercultural Perspectives.* Reprinted by permission of Meridian House International, Washington, DC. Copyright 1975 by Meridian House International.

Griggs Productions. Examples in Resource 7 from *Going International Part 5, Working in the USA*, and *Going International Part 6, Living in the USA.* Used by permission of Griggs Productions, San Francisco. Copyright 1986 by Griggs Productions.

The authors were unable to locate the publisher or author of the following:

Lord, E. Case study from *Examples of Cross-Cultural Problems Encountered by Americans Working Overseas: An Instructor's Handbook.* Alexandria, VA: HumRRO, 1965.

Scarangello, Anthony, ed. For thirteen examples from *American Education through Foreign Eyes.* Copyright 1967 by Hobbs, Dorman, New York.

The authors further wish to express their gratitude to the following people:

Michael L. G. Berney of Berney Associates Training and Organization Development, Silver Spring, Maryland (formerly of Washington International Center), for contributing the ideas in Resources 1A, 5, 6A, 6B, and 9B, and for help in editing the original manuscript, especially Appendix A.

Kay T. C. Clifford of the International Center of the University of Michigan for permission to use the Surprise Introduction (Resource 3), for the alternatives in Resource 9A, and for a case study in Resource 16.

Sandra Mumford Fowler for permission to use the exercise in Resource 1B, the adaptation of "Cultural Encounter" in Resource 14, and ideas for the evaluation.

Dr. Francis L. K. Hsu for his comparison of American and Chinese cultural assumptions which contributed to Kohls's development of his list of "Cultural Truths" of Americans (Resource 6A). This work appeared in *The Study of Literate Civilizations*, published by Holt, Rinehart & Winston, New York, 1969 (out of print).

IPI editors for their usual meticulous job in editing the final manuscript.

Alan Kotak, President of Overseas Technology, Inc., Arlington, Virginia, for validating the Evaluation Form.

Dr. Alfred J. Kraemer of the Human Resources Research Organization (HumRRO), Alexandria, Virginia, for ideas contributing to the development of Kohls's list of "Cultural Truths" (Resource 6A). Kraemer's work was reported in *Intercultural Sourcebook*, published by SIETAR International in 1979. A more complete description of Kraemer's work may be found in *Development of a Cultural Self-Awareness Approach to Instruction in Intercultural Communication* (Technical Report 73-17; HumRRO, Alexandria, Virginia, 1973).

Mobley, Luciani & Associates for permission to use ideas contained in their Value Option Cards in the development of Cross-Cultural Values Cards (Resource 6).

Barbara Steinwachs for permission to use much of the material in Appendix A.

V. Lynn Tyler, Brigham Young University, for permission to use many of the case studies appearing in Resource 16, the additional information sections in other case studies, and invaluable help in revision of the original manuscript.

Dr. Charles Vetter for permission to use example 34 in Resource 7.

Preface

There is, in these last years of the twentieth century, no more noble calling than to help the people of the world live together in peace and understanding with a fully developed spirit of inquiry about other cultures and other ways. This is not an easy quest and requires all of us to become fully aware of our own cultural conditioning and fully cognizant of the assumptions and values that lie outside our awareness but influence every part of our conscious lives. It also requires that we build some skill in developing and maintaining relationships with people from cultures different, sometimes dramatically different, from our own. The material in this book is designed to assist in that task.

This is a simple book, a how-to book. It demonstrates how to lead a workshop designed to develop intercultural awareness in a culturally naive audience. Although it is a basic how-to book, it assumes some intercultural knowledge and some facilitation skill in the trainer, teacher, or facilitator who uses the material. If the potential facilitator feels that additional knowledge is needed, we recommend that the books listed in Appendix C be read and absorbed. Less experienced workshop leaders may find it useful to work with someone who is experienced. An individual may also obtain training through the professional development opportunities that exist in the field of cross-cultural training.

Throughout the late sixties and the early seventies a major debate in the intercultural field centered around whether cross-cultural training should be "country- or culture-specific" or "culture-general." That is, should training focus only on a particular country, or should it be designed to help people develop skills useful in any intercultural situation? The unstated assumption was that the two approaches were mutually exclusive. Fortunately the debate was eventually resolved, with very little fanfare, in favor of including *both* approaches. It has become common practice to start with culture-general material and exercises, then turn to the culture of one's own country (in our case, this means exploring the culture of the United States), and, finally, to include a country-specific phase that concentrates on the country to which the participants are going. This book concerns itself largely with the first phase—the culture-general—with some attention to the culture of the United States. Those conducting intercultural awareness workshops may want to add a culture-specific segment that addresses the interests and needs of particular participant groups. The workshop design certainly lends itself to this possibility.

Culture-general exercises can also be used alone to increase workshop participants' awareness of the cultural issues that are an integral part of relationships between those who are culturally different. This is the case, for example, when the goal of the training is to increase participants' understanding of those who are ethnically and culturally different, or to deal with and reduce the level of counterproductive stereotypes or prejudices. It is also useful as a general program for a group of people who may be traveling on assignment to a variety of countries or who will be managing, from the home office, Americans working in different locations around the world.

As the diversity of the U.S. work force has become increasingly apparent, culture-general exercises have been used with managers and staff of different ethnic and cultural backgrounds. In this sense *Developing Intercultural Awareness* has multiple applications, limited only by the facilitator's imagination. We urge you to adapt the activities freely and to create your own version of any of the exercises to fit specific needs and groups. There is no single right way.

If it hadn't been for John Knight, the revision of this book would never have been accomplished. Although incredibly busy, John provided the energy and more than his share of the ideas for the revised *Developing Intercultural Awareness*. The collaboration has been a fortuitous one, and it is with pride that I share the authorship with him. I personally hope that this effort has been as fulfilling for him as it has been for me. I hope, too, that it will spur him on to writing books of his own, the ideas for which are kicking around in his head just waiting to come out.

L. Robert Kohls
San Francisco

Preface

In 1967 I chose the Peace Corps and Ethiopia, and that one choice has shaped my life. After three months of immersion training, both in the U.S. and Ethiopia, I was to spend three years teaching in a rural school. Little did I realize that those three years would barely scratch the surface of the beginning of cultural understanding. During my stint as a teacher, I wrote and later revised an eighth-grade world history text in an effort to provide my students with a book that was simple to understand and culturally relevant to their experience. Yet when Bob Kohls asked me to revise the first edition of his *Developing Intercultural Awareness*, the meaning of what such a revision would entail did not hit me until I was well into the project, by which time there was no backing out. As with my Peace Corps experience, I was hooked.

This expanded second edition includes the work of many intercultural trainers. The exercises have been used in a variety of settings, including business and academia. I feel privileged to have worked with as patient and understanding a mentor as Bob Kohls. We trust you will find this edition useful and, above all, enjoyable.

John M. Knight
San Francisco

General Considerations

Developing Intercultural Awareness

1. Expected Audience

   These workshops are designed for adults who may be considered to be culturally naive. They have been used successfully with American business-people and their spouses, military officers, teachers, graduate-level university students, Peace Corps volunteers, foreign service officers, and missionaries. Many of the exercises have been used with a vast array of participant groups in the American domestic as well as international environments. In fact, if the participant group includes a cross-section of ethnic and cultural representatives that make up the society of the U.S., this diversity is a rich resource. Facilitators will want to tap this resource whenever possible. While participation by foreign nationals can also provide cross-cultural enrichment to this workshop, it has not been designed for a mixed audience of Americans and foreign nationals, nor is it intended for audiences composed exclusively of foreign nationals.

2. Objectives

   These workshops are designed to:

   a. Increase positive attitudes toward the people of other countries and cultures.

   b. Increase awareness of the problems that arise in communicating with people of other cultures.

   c. Increase awareness of participants' own American cultural values and unstated cultural assumptions.

   d. Call attention to any counterproductive stereotypes and prejudices toward people of other cultures.

   e. Assist in preparing people to better adapt to and be more productive during an overseas living experience.

3. Materials and resources required

   A variety of exercises are included in the materials for these workshops. Alternatives to the primary resource are labeled A, B, and C. The facilitator(s) should decide which one(s) will best meet the needs of a particular workshop.

The materials needed are listed at the beginning of each resource; in general, you should have at your disposal:

- an overhead projector and transparencies, or slide projector and slides (prepared in advance)
- screen or suitable wall surface
- flip chart(s) or blackboard and magic markers/chalk
- movable chairs (to allow participants to move into different groups)
- handouts as called for in the description of the activity. Time the distribution of these so the workshop flow is maintained.

4. Number of participants

   These workshop designs have been used successfully with from ten to sixty participants; about twenty is the most desirable group size. Obviously, group size must be considered when selecting activities and deciding how they will be conducted. The time recommended for each activity is an estimate and will vary from facilitator to facilitator and with the size of the group. It is useful to go in to any workshop with alternative activities on hand. Sometimes it is necessary to abandon an exercise and substitute another when the first choice is not working with a particular group. At other times, the group may move through the material more quickly than anticipated, and the facilitator must be prepared to keep the group engaged using backup resources and the available time to elaborate on the concepts that are being explored.

5. Room Requirements

   Room size must correspond to the size of the group. Movable chairs, which will allow multiple groupings, are a necessity. Well-lit, sunny rooms have a definite psychological advantage over dark or windowless rooms. Some exercises require that a second (adjacent or nearby) room be available for break-out groups.

6. Workshop Design

   A detailed two-day workshop design is included in this volume as well as an abbreviated one-day plan. Facilitators should feel free to adapt either plan to their own needs. Breaks, except for the exercise "Bingo Break," have not been built in to the designs, but are left to the discretion of the facilitator(s).

Workshop Design
Two-day

Time	Activity	Training Purpose
DAY 1		
10-20 mins.	Welcome: ■ Brief self-introduction by facilitator ■ Icebreaker activity (see Resources 1/1A/1B/1C)	Opening and establishing credibility Establish a climate of group participation in examining cultural values

Transition: *After exploring the expectations of participants and facilitator(s), introduce the workshop objectives in a way that refers to and reinforces or "corrects" the expectations that have been expressed.*

Time	Activity	Training Purpose
15-20 mins.	■ Expectations of both facilitator and participants (see Resource 2) ■ Presentation of objectives (see #2 in General Considerations)	
30 mins.	Intercultural Introductions: ■ If twenty or fewer, have the participants, one by one, introduce themselves as cross-cultural beings; ask them to stress any cross-cultural experience(s) they have had, any cultural or ethnic groups of which they are members, and any needs they have to improve their intercultural awareness ■ Facilitator introduces him- or herself this way *first*, as an example (see Resource 3 for alternative introduction to use if group is larger than 20)	Initial Activity: Individual presentations to get to know each other; information sharing Learning the total cultural experiences and needs of the group Modeling; establishing credibility Modeling U.S. values

Time	Activity	Training Purpose

Transition: *The next exercise is an introduction to just how "natural" our cultural baggage is and how we can develop an awareness of our ethnocentrism.*

Time	Activity	Training Purpose
30-45 mins.	Reaching Consensus: ■ See Resource 4 for description of exercise ■ Give instructions ■ Individual scoring	Group Activity: To point out fallacies and biases in *all* these too commonly held attitudes (but facilitator should not reveal the fact that *all* statements need changing)
	■ Discussion to make changes ■ Record written statements within each group	
	■ Have each group report orally	To let peers do the teaching; to provide opportunity for facilitator to underscore a number of key points as they come up in discussions which accompany the oral reports

Transition: *The purpose of the following short lecture, or "lecturette," is to continue the process of building awareness of our ethnocentrism and stereotypical thinking from a more theoretical perspective.*

Time	Activity	Training Purpose
25 mins.	Lecturette: ■ See pp. 13-20, *Survival Kit for Overseas Living* (citation in Appendix C) ■ Ask participants to define "civilization" or "civilized"	Listening: Awareness of ethnocentrism
	■ Demonstrate danger of a widespread Western concept ("Civilized"/ "Primitive") ■ Present the diagram	Unlearning cultural prejudices and stereotypes

Civilized

Primitive

■ Culture concept

Time	Activity	Training Purpose

Transition: *The purpose of the Bingo Break is to continue to build group cohesion using cultural cues while taking a break that allows everyone to move around the room.*

| 20 mins. | ■ Bingo Break (see Resource 5) | Building group cohesion |

Transition: *The following lecturette continues the awareness-building process by using a theoretical model which contrasts middle-class American values with those of other cultures.*

| 20 mins. | Lecturette:
■ A relatively bias-free way of comparing cultures (present the chart of the Kluckhohn Model)
■ See pp. 21-26, *Survival Kit for Overseas Living* for content
■ Explain and show where American middle-class values fall as well as those of any U.S. ethnic groups represented in the group
■ Indicate where other cultures' values fall | Explanation of Model: Awareness of appropriate (unbiased) ways to compare and contrast cultures

Awareness of fundamental differences between cultures |
| 45-60 mins. | LUNCH | |

Transition: *This morning we looked at some counterproductive stereotypes and prejudices which we might have about people of other cultures. This afternoon we will examine American values as they contrast with values in other countries.*

| 40 mins. | Cross-Cultural Value Cards:
■ See Resource 6 for instructions
■ See Resources 6A and 6B for alternatives | Interaction and practice in identifying a variety of cultural orientations |

Transition: *Now that we have a better understanding of what we as Americans are like, we need to examine how others perceive us, i.e., some common stereotypes about Americans.*

Time	Activity	Training Purpose
20 mins.	■ Explore reactions to observations by foreign visitors about Americans ■ See Resource 7 for instructions ■ As an alternative, see Appendix B for description of *Cold Water* video	Group activity involves questioning why we do things the way we do Practice explaining and defending why we do what we do, looking for the logic behind our actions; looking at ourselves from a different viewpoint

Transition: *Go on to foreigners' stereotypes of Americans. Based on what you now know about cultural values and ethnocentrism, how do you think these stereotypes evolve?*

Time	Activity	Training Purpose
20 mins.	■ Stereotypes of Americans held by foreigners ■ Show Duane Hanson's sculpture of *Tourists* (source: *Survival Kit for Overseas Living*, p. 4) ■ Brainstorm stereotypes commonly held of Americans by foreigners ■ See Resource 8 for instructions ■ See *Survival Kit for Overseas Living*, pp. 5-7	Attention-getting Deepening awareness that cultural biases often lead to stereotyping

Transition: *What are some of the American values that we exhibit through our actions, media, etc. that lead to these stereotypes?*

Time	Activity	Training Purpose
20 mins.	■ Discovering American values through American proverbs: "What are American values?" ■ Difficult to answer, even though we have all been thoroughly enculturated into them as Americans ■ Easy to discover—through American proverbs and axioms	To make participants aware of American values, how difficult they are to identify, and how easy it is to retrieve them through our proverbs Other countries' proverbs can also reveal their values which may or may not be similar to American values

Time	Activity	Training Purpose
	■ See Resource 9 for instructions ■ See Resources 9A and 9B for alternatives	

Transition: *What questions do the participants have at the close of the first day?*

Time	Activity	Training Purpose
20 mins.	■ Questions or relevant comments ■ Hand out reading assignment—"Body Ritual among the Nacirema" (see Appendix C)	Questions, answers, discussion Preparation for next day
10 mins.	Reflective Mirror: ■ See Resource 13 for instructions	Closure: Final group exercise in which participants again do something new

DAY 2

Time	Activity	Training Purpose
10 mins.	■ Welcome ■ Review of previous day	Set the stage for activities of day two

Transition: *How do the different perceptions discussed during day one illustrate the various ways the communication (our next topic) was received?*

Time	Activity	Training Purpose
25 mins.	Communication: ■ Introduction and discussion of five points of communication from Pierre Casse (see Resource 10)	Introduce the idea of communication and its impact on cross-cultural interactions

Transition: *How does communication affect the ways in which the Martian Anthropology Exercise is carried out?*

Time	Activity	Training Purpose
60-120 mins.	Martian Anthropology Exercise: ■ See Resource 11 for instructions ■ Time for exercise will depend on size of group and site (see Appendix A for alternative simulations)	To give the participants a chance to use what they learned in day one, gain a different perspective on American culture, and try something new—which simulates cross-cultural interaction

Time	Activity	Training Purpose
60-90 mins.	LUNCH	Includes time for groups to prepare reports
60-90 mins.	■ Martian Anthropology Exercise reports and debriefing ■ See instructions for options for discussion ■ If the Martian Anthropology Exercise is not run, a case study or a movie may be substituted during this time block (see Resource 16 and Appendix B). What the facilitator uses will depend on the composition of the group and its willingness to engage in experiential learning.	Group Activity: Allows for discussion of exercise

Transition: *What tools can we use to continue our cross-cultural development when we are overseas or involved with a multicultural work group in the U.S.? A cross-cultural journal can help.*

Time	Activity	Training Purpose
15 mins.	■ Cross-Cultural Journal (see Resource 12 for description)	A way to continue individual learning in a new setting
10 mins.	■ Suggestions for further reading, extensive bibliographies, and area studies resources (see Appendix C)	Where to go for more in-depth information

Transition: *What have you learned in the past two days? What more do you need to learn? How can you as individuals and as a group continue this learning?*

Time	Activity	Training Purpose
15-20 mins.	■ Group analysis of main points covered in workshop ■ Participants, not the facilitator, do the summing up ■ Ask question—What was American about this workshop? ■ Facilitator jots ideas down on flip chart ■ Fill out evaluation	Summary To reinforce the idea that what we do, even in designing a workshop, reflects our culture

Time	Activity	Training Purpose
5 mins.	Reflective Mirror: ■ See Resource 13 for directions	Closure

N.B. Day one takes approximately seven hours, including breaks. Day two can take from four and a half hours to seven hours, depending on the size of the group and the exercises chosen.

Workshop Design
One-day

■ The following lesson plan can be used for one-day training programs. For explanations of activities, refer to the two-day lesson plan. Facilitators are encouraged to adapt this lesson plan (5 ½ to 6 hours) to their own needs.

Time	Activity
10-20 mins.	Welcome Icebreaker—Resources 1/1A/1B/1C
15-20 mins.	Expectations
30 mins.	Intercultural Introductions
30-45 mins.	Reaching Consensus
20 mins.	Break (Bingo Break can be used if appropriate)
25 mins.	Lecturette (see pp. 13-20, *Survival Kit for Overseas Living*—Appendix C for source)
45-60 mins.	LUNCH
75 mins.	*Cold Water* video—Appendix B for description, or a case study from Resource 16 together with Observations of Foreign Visitors—Resource 7, or "The Sacred Rac"—see *Learning about Peoples and Cultures* in Appendix C for source.
20 mins.	American Values—Resources 9/9A/9B
30 mins.	Cultural Encounter—Resource 14
10 mins.	Cross-Cultural Journal—Resource 12
10 mins.	Suggestions for Further Reading—Appendix C
15 mins.	Group's Analysis of Main Points Covered in Workshop
15 mins.	Evaluation
5 mins.	Reflective Mirror—Resource 13

Resource 1

Icebreaker—Push/Pull*

- Goals: To develop an awareness of the importance of physical (kinesthetic) sensitivity and to help establish group cohesiveness.
- Group size: Six to sixty people. Works best with medium-sized groups.
- Materials: Cassette tape recorder and recording of a piece of dramatic, flowing music of three to four minutes in length such as the theme song from *Chariots of Fire* by Vangelis.

Procedure

Demonstrate the different tasks the participants will perform during the exercise.

1. Instruct participants to walk around the room as the music plays and to listen for directions.

   a. First, tell them to form pairs and to stand face-to-face with arms up, bent at the elbow, hands open, palms out, with fingers pointing up (typical "hands-up" pose). Then, instruct them to push against their partner's palms and try to find a "balance" in their pushing, so that they are supported, and neither one is overpowered by the other. They can try different levels by stretching, bending their knees, or leaning from side to side.

   b. Second, when you call "Break and Pull," both partners should stop pushing, hold hands (left hand to partner's right and right to partner's left), and begin to pull away from each other, again trying to find a balance.

   c. Third, when you call "Break and Walk," the participants leave their partners and walk around the room.

   d. Fourth, instruct them to form groups of three (or whatever number will allow all people to be in a group), and to repeat the push/pull sequence they just did in pairs. It may be more difficult to achieve a balance since more than two people are involved.

   e. Last, if the size of the group and room permit, have everyone form one large circle for the push/pull sequence finale.

2. Begin the discussion by asking how the exercise relates to the workshop. By brainstorming this first question, issues related to space, touching, and other culture-based differences in nonverbal communication can be introduced.

The relationship between physical sensitivity and cultural sensitivity may also be fruitfully explored with questions related to personal and cultural reactions to the exercise. Were participants able to develop a balance in the push/pull, or was one person more or less active or forceful in the exercise? You can also point out that this kind of warm-up is different from the usual icebreaker and may test the participants' tolerance for ambiguity. Some audiences (e.g., business executives) may find this type of exercise too "touchy-feely"; the facilitator needs to assess the audience carefully before using it.

---

*Contributed by John M. Knight.

Resource 1A

Icebreaker—Examine the Room*

- Goal: To demonstrate quickly how culture affects all we do.
- Group size: Variable. Make sure that there are a few more chairs than there are participants.

Procedure

1. Ask the group to observe where people are sitting. What spaces are left? How closely are they seated? What are the characteristics of the groupings of people who are sitting near each other? What materials or possessions did people bring/not bring? What assumptions do people have about the kind of interaction that is going to occur today? Where did those assumptions originate?

2. Relate this to the workshop's general goal of cultural awareness. Explain that one of the objectives for the workshop is to make us more aware of assumptions that we make that arise from our cultural background as Americans, for example, how our concept of physical space affects the distance we seat ourselves from others.

---

*Contributed by Michael L. G. Berney.

Resource 1B

Icebreaker—Draw a House*

- Goal: To understand the effects of cultural conditioning on people's ability to do a task.
- Group size: Variable.
- Materials: Pen and paper.

Procedure

1. Ask participants to select a partner as different from themselves as possible.
2. Then ask each two-person team to share a single pen or pencil and, with both persons holding the pen at the same time, draw a house on a blank sheet of paper. Talking is permitted.
3. After two to three minutes, ask them to stop, turn the paper over and, without talking, draw a house together from a uniquely different culture, e.g., an igloo. The type of house will depend on the composition of your group. Give them three to four minutes to do the task.
4. Allow the teams to present and talk about their houses. Then ask:
   - How did you draw your house?
   - What were the barriers to doing the task?
   - Did talking help or hinder?
   - In what ways were you aware of the relationship with your partner? How did it feel to lead/follow?
   - What happens in your life that this reminds you of?
   - How can you use what you learned here?
5. Close the exercise by discussing how our cultural conditioning leads us to view situations in predetermined ways and to respond to tasks in ways appropriate to one culture. Even when our cultures do not share the same expectations about a situation, a cooperative task can be accomplished if we stay alert to our cultural differences, check understanding, and learn to communicate.

---

*Contributed by Sandra Mumford Fowler. Original design by Paul Pedersen.

Resource 1C

Icebreaker[1]—The Form[2]

- Goal: To understand the effects of cultural conditioning on people's ability to do a task.
- Group size: Variable.
- Materials: One copy of The Form (see p. 19) for each participant and a few 3 x 5 white index cards with green magic marker lines drawn on them. There should also be a flip chart or blackboard available for the discussion period.

Procedure

This exercise has a dual purpose. Initially, it can be used as a different kind of icebreaker to shock the participants into an awareness of how different cultures are and how visceral our reactions to these differences can be. Later on, the information recorded from the participants' reactions can be used as realistic examples to accompany those provided in the Reaching Consensus Exercise in Resource 4.

1. Distribute copies of The Form and the green-and-white cards. Each participant should receive a copy of The Form; the green and-white cards should only be given to a select few. Then, read the following inflexible rules.

   - Write from right to left.
   - Write very clearly. Sloppy writing will be discarded.
   - Fill in every blank.
   - For #2 use the Moslem calendar, which begins July 16, A.D. 622.
   - Do not answer #7 unless you have a green-and-white card.
   - Complete this task within three minutes.
   - Ask no questions!

2. The initial discussion should focus on the participants' personal and cultural reactions to the exercise. Ask the participants how they felt during the exercise and record their responses, using single words or short phrases, on a flip chart or blackboard. Why did some use descriptions like "backwards," "stupid," or "frustrating," rather than "right to left" or "opposite from the way I usually write" to describe how they felt? This idea of which words we use to describe things can be further discussed during the Reaching Consensus Exercise found in Resource 4.

Additional questions can include:

- What does the word "blank" mean in the instructions, since there are both blank *lines* and blank *spaces*?
- Did the information about the Moslem calendar cause any problems?
- Was any of the information on the form confusing?
- Did the questions make sense? Why do you think they were asked? If you wanted to get to know someone, what questions would you ask?
- How many people actually finished the form?
- How did people cope with completing the form? In other words, who held the paper up to the light backward to read it, who wrote left to right, and who just gave up?

Remember to keep the discussion open and free-flowing.

3. Close the exercise by discussing how we are culturally conditioned to view situations in predetermined ways and to respond to tasks in ways appropriate to our culture, as well as how we obtain information and how confused we are by other ways of doing so.

THE FORM

1. NAME _____
FAMILY??
BIRTH

2. YEARS _____

3. SEX   YES _____
NO _____

4. STATUS

5. DEGREES
CHECKONEO,Y,X
PHD
PDQ
AM
MA
PM

6. FAVORITE COLOR
_____
WHY? _____

7. LANGUAGE
YES ___   NO _____

8. [E]NGLISH
WHATKIND
KOJAK
REGAN
EDITH

9. FAVORITEDISEASE

Resource 2

Expectations*

- Goal: To have both facilitator and participants discuss their expectations of the workshop.
- Group size: Variable.
- Materials: Paper (or newsprint) and pens/pencils; flip chart.

Procedure

This exercise works well with small groups and with larger groups divided into subgroups of five to fifteen to discuss and report back to the whole group.

1. Instruct participants to record their thoughts quickly on two sheets of paper (or newsprint if in small groups) as follows:

   a. On one sheet, they write their expectations for themselves in the workshop (what they hope to learn, how they plan to behave, etc.) and, in a second column, their expectations of the facilitator (what attributes they expect in a facilitator, how they expect her/him to behave, etc.).

   b. On the second sheet, they write what they think the facilitator expects of them as a group and, in a second column, what they think the facilitator expects of her- or himself.

2. Do the same exercise on a flip chart from a facilitator's perspective.

3. Review the perceptions as a group and tie them in with the objectives of the workshop. Are participants and/or the facilitator willing to give up any of these expectations to improve group cohesiveness and further the aims of the workshop? These expectations can be taped up on the wall and kept in view during the workshop, if desired.

4. During the final evaluation of the entire workshop, bring out these expectation sheets to see how they were met (or not met).

---

*Contributed by John M. Knight.

Resource 3

Surprise Introduction*

- Goal: To highlight cultural differences at the outset of the workshop.
- Group size: Variable. Works best with small groups.
- Materials: Pen and paper.

Procedure

1. Explain that, as the facilitator, you will be departing from tradition and introducing yourself last.

2. Ask participants to write down the most important thing about themselves in twenty-five words or less; specifically, write what they would want people to remember about them after they are dead.

3. Have the participants read their introductions aloud one by one. If the group is large, select only a few to read. (Those unread can be contrasted later with the facilitator's introduction.)

4. Next, introduce yourself using the following model of a relationship-oriented introduction: "My name is John Doe. My father is Jeremiah Doe and is a native of Massachusetts. He is a country lawyer who specializes in family law. My mother is Judith Alexander Doe. Her parents were the well-known Mr. and Mrs. Edsel Doe of the car business. My mother is a housewife in Peoria, Massachusetts. I have a brother, Eldereth Doe, who is a corporate lawyer in upstate New York. I also have a sister, Elaindra Doe, who is a housewife and mother of four. My wife, Carol Smithe Doe, is the daughter of Mr. and Mrs. Arthur Smithe, who reside in Michigan. I have three children, two sons and one daughter."

   Note: Use your own example and base it entirely on real relationships, if possible. When people begin to squirm during the introduction, keep going a little longer and then stop.

5. Have participants compare your introduction with theirs, which were probably more job- or role-oriented. The discussion should focus on how introductions reflect cultural values. For instance, in a culture in which relationships are highly valued, one would introduce oneself, as the facilitator did, in terms of family name and relationships. What part of the country a person is from and the school(s) attended may be important in some cultures in order to place a person in the "proper" role. In the United States, where emphasis is

placed on achievement, what a person "does" is often the main concern in an introduction. Thus, cultures structure reality differently, and this structure can be discerned through an awareness of how behaviors (e.g., introductions) differ.

---

*Developed by Kay T. C. Clifford.

Resource 4

Reaching Consensus*

- Goal: To introduce participants to the subconscious ethnocentrism which pervades our daily lives.
- Group size: Variable.
- Materials: Photocopies of p. 27.

Procedure

1. Divide the group into subgroups of three to five and give them the following instructions:

    - *Individually*, place an "A" or a "D" beside each statement on the sheet to indicate whether you *personally agree* (A) or *disagree* (D) with it.

    - Then, going over each statement in order, check to see if *anyone* in your group disagrees with it. If even one person disagrees, the group should change the wording so that the statement is acceptable, as reworded, to *all* members of the group. The same applies when *everyone* in the group disagrees with a statement: it must be changed so as to make it acceptable.

    - You *may not* simply "agree to disagree."

    - Choose one member to record the revised, acceptable statements.

2. Report orally. Ask each group to report on a couple of the statements, and ask for alternate revisions from other groups.

3. If time is limited or if the group is exceptionally large, it's a good idea to assign one or two statements to each subgroup, so that all the statements can be covered in a shorter time. Another alternative is to ask some subgroups to start from the top of the list while others start from the bottom.

The value of this exercise lies not so much in whether or not the statements per se are valid, but in the discussions they spark. In particular, the exercise allows participants to learn more from their enlightened peers than from an "authority" on the subject. It also provides the facilitator with the opportunity to underscore certain key points, especially how pervasive ethnocentrism is and how difficult it is to form nonjudgmental or nonethnocentric statements.

4. Ask group members to identify ethnocentric attitudes demonstrated in the statements.

5. Explore how the groups reached consensus on the rewording of the statements and what attitudes were challenged in the process.

----

*Developed by L. Robert Kohls.

Attachment to Resource 4

_____ 1. The fact that the first man on the moon was an Amercan is proof of America's technological superiority.

_____ 2. Foreigners going to live in a new country should let go of their own culture and adapt to the new country as quickly as possible.

_____ 3. Orientals do many things backwards.

_____ 4. Many Third World countries are "underdeveloped" through lack of initiative on the part of their inhabitants.

_____ 5. Everyone should learn English as it is the one unifying language.

_____ 6. The Vietnamese do not place as much value on human life as Americans do.

_____ 7. Americans have been very generous in teaching other people how to do things the right way.

_____ 8. Primitive people have not yet reached the higher stages of civilization.

_____ 9. Minority members of a population should conform to the customs and values of the majority.

_____ 10. Other people in the world should learn to do things the way Americans do, so that we will all be able to understand each other better.

Resource 5

Bingo Break*

- Goal: To build group cohesion using cultural cues.
- Group size: Variable.
- Materials: Pen and paper.
- Advance preparation: Prepare a grid (or use the one on p. 31) with five squares across and five squares down. Then fill in the squares with cues (see below) and include a few free spaces as most bingo cards do.

Procedure

1. Hand out one card to each participant. Allow them twenty minutes to mingle and fill out the squares on the cards with the names of participants who fit the descriptions. Any given participant may not be used to fill in more than one item (this can vary depending on group size). The first person to complete the card (or the person with the most squares completed) within the time period wins.

2. Here is a sample list of cues:
   - has read Edward T. Hall's *The Silent Language*
   - speaks Spanish
   - knows how many points you get for a soccer goal
   - knows what *nisei* means
   - has listened to a non-English-speaking radio station
   - has eaten Korean food in the past three months
   - has a close friend from a different culture
   - has never left his or her home state
   - comes from an intercultural family
   - knows who Carlos Salinas de Gortari (or some other prominent international person) is
   - has five or more brothers and sisters
   - knows what country Alex Haley based his book *Roots* on
   - is wearing something of cultural significance
   - can speak two languages besides English

- knows who wrote *Custer Died for Your Sins*
- has lived one or more years outside the United States
- did not eat breakfast this morning
- is left-handed
- plays guitar
- loves broccoli

Culture Cue Bingo

INSTRUCTIONS: Distribute "Culture Cue Bingo" grid sheets and pencils to each participant.

Participants must approach others in the group to get them to "sign off," i.e., write their name, in a particular square of the grid whose category they can fulfill. If some people know each other, suggest they seek out strangers.

Participants continue to fill in the grid with others in the group until they have completed a full column, row, or diagonal.

Participants may only use each name once or twice and must have group members sign their own name on the grid sheet.

The purpose of the exercise is to get people to meet each other. You might also ask if they found anything that surprised them, intrigued them, or made them want to learn more about the person in question.

---

*Contributed by Michael L. G. Berney.

Culture Cue
BINGO

INSTRUCTIONS: Get signatures of people who fit the descriptions in the boxes. Limit—two signatures per person.

Resource 6

Cross-Cultural Value Cards*

- Goals: To increase group interaction and to practice identifying a variety of cultural orientations.
- Group size: Fifteen to fifty people. Works best with large, heterogeneous groups.
- Advance preparation: See attached sheets for three sets of value statements (forty-five in number) to be typed separately on 3 x 5 index cards, one value per card; or photocopy the statements, cut the boxes apart, and paste them on index cards, one per card.

Procedure

1. Pass out eight randomly selected cards to each person in the room. (Prepare enough duplicates to have a total of eight cards per person.)
2. Instruct participants to trade their cards to *upgrade* them (upgrade=get values they prefer). Each participant must end up with no fewer than two cards (this means each may trade more than one card for one he/she particularly wants). Keep this to ten to fifteen minutes so participants can't chitchat too much.
3. Have participants pair up with other members of the group whose values are *compatible* with their own. Discuss what they have in common. Again, keep the time for this short.
4. Disband the compatible groups and instruct each participant to pair up with another person whose values are *opposite* his/her own. Assignment: prepare a new statement of values for each card they hold (or a selected number of cards) with which both can agree.
5. Ask for sample compromise statements which can be written on a flip chart. The goal here is not to gather all the compromise statements, but simply to elicit some examples. Further discussion can focus on the ability to/necessity of compromise in intercultural situations. The facilitator can also ask the participants to select ten to fifteen typical American value statements to be listed on the flip chart. The component values for each statement can then be contrasted with "Other Cultural Values" (see Resource 6B for list of American and "other" cultural values).
6. Variations on this basic exercise can include having half the group collect values their grandparents held while the other half collects values of modern-

day Americans. Other contrasting value sets might include personal values versus typical American values, or Third World values versus American values. The rest of the instructions would remain the same.

7. The following explanation of the A-E categories of the value cards is adapted from *Survival Kit for Overseas Living* by L. Robert Kohls.

A=Human Nature Orientation—the innate character of human nature

B=Human to Nature Orientation—the proper relationship of people to nature

C=Time Orientation—the temporal focus of human life

D=Activity Orientation—how people profitably occupy themselves

E=Social Orientation—the proper relationship of an individual to other people

---

*Developed by L. Robert Kohls. Keyed to values on the Kluckhohn Model.[3] Based on similar Value Option Cards activities invented by Mobley, Luciani & Associates.

Cross-Cultural Value Cards[4]—Set 1

	1	2	3
A	Most people can't be trusted.	There are both evil people and good people in the world and you have to check to find out which are which.	Most people are basically pretty good at heart.
B	Life is largely determined by external forces, such as God or Fate. A person can't surpass the conditions life has set.	Humans should, in every way, live in complete harmony with nature.	The human challenge is to conquer and control nature. Everything from air conditioning to the "green revolution" has resulted from our having met this challenge.
C	Humans should learn from history and attempt to emulate the glorious ages of the past.	The present moment is everything. Let's make the most of it. Don't worry about tomorrow, enjoy today.	Planning and goal setting make it possible for humans to accomplish miracles. A little sacrifice today will bring a better tomorrow.
D	It's not necessary to accomplish great things in life to feel your life has been worthwhile. It's enough just to "be."	Human beings' main purpose for being placed on this earth is for their own inner development.	If people work hard and apply themselves fully, their efforts will be rewarded.
E	Some people are born to lead others. There are "leaders" and there are "followers" in this world.	Whenever I have a serious problem, I like to get the advice of my family or close friends on how best to solve it.	All people should have equal rights as well as complete control over their own destinies.

Cross-Cultural Value Cards—Set 2

	1	2	3
A	We need jails and prisons because people have an inclination toward evil. Some people are born criminals.	There will always be people who will extend a helping hand, and there will also be those who will try to chop yours off.	A person should always be considered innocent until proven guilty.
B	Humans cannot surpass the conditions life has set. What will be will be.	Humans should never do anything to pollute their precious earth.	Humans are nature's greatest accomplishment, and they have rightly been assigned the task of controlling and perfecting nature.
C	I look back with fondness on the days of my childhood. Those were the happiest days of my life.	Be here now, for tomorrow is uncertain and yesterday is but a memory.	You should plan ahead for the unexpected by putting aside a little money for a "rainy day."
D	To love is better than to do; to be is better than to have.	It's more important to pay attention to your inner development than to try to get ahead in life.	To achieve anything, you have to at least make an effort. Anything worth having is worth working for.
E	In times of difficulty, it's best to go to someone who has the power to change the situation and ask for help.	The most satisfying and effective form of decision making is group consensus.	Any society which does not allow individuals to voice their dissent is not a free society.

Cross-Cultural Value Cards—Set 3

	1	2	3
A	You've got to constantly look out for your own welfare. If you don't look out for yourself, no one else will.	When your children are young, train them in the right ways. Left alone, they can go wrong just as easily as right.	There's always someone who will lend a helping hand when you're in need.
B	A person made humble by acknowledging her/his own inferiority to the elements is more powerful than one who challenges them.	Each person is but one component of nature and should, at all times, respect the integrity of all other forms of life.	All natural resources were placed on this earth to be at people's disposal.
C	Who needs day-care centers? Mothers and grandmothers have been taking care of children for thousands of years and doing a fine job.	Live every day as if it were the only day that counts.	Wise people map out their plans for the future; they know what they want to be doing five, ten, and twenty years from now.
D	People's importance stems from their mere existence and not from any acts they perform.	Do not look outward, but concern yourself only with the world within.	The happy person is the one who never sits still but who is constantly involved in productive activity.
E	One should follow the requests of one's superiors without questioning their authority.	Luckily, we don't have to stand on our own. We have the group to support and sustain us.	The creative tension which competition provides is healthy and brings out the best in each individual.

Resource 6A

Cultural Values*

- Goal: To identify those implicit cultural assumptions unique to a region or subculture of the United States and those common to Americans in general.
- Group size: Variable.
- Materials: Flip charts and sets of markers.
- Advance preparation: Set up the room so that there will be groups of four to five people seated in semicircles facing flip charts posted on the wall or on easels around the perimeter of the room. Write the following instructions on the blackboard or a separate flip chart:
  - As you enter the room, identify and sit with people who have a background similar to your own, in terms of region of origin, ethnicity/national background, etc.
  - Write the name of your identifying characteristic at the top of your flip chart.

    Note: These instructions are deliberately ambiguous, requiring participants to use a little imagination in dividing themselves up in a workable fashion.

Procedure

1. Explain to everyone in the room that the purpose of this exercise is to identify those implicit cultural assumptions that are unique to a subculture or region of the United States and those that are common to Americans in general. You will distribute to each group a list of "cultural truths of Americans" and a set of markers so that they can write down examples of those truths that apply to them on their lists.

2. Background on Cultural Truths: These "cultural truths" are beliefs which lie so deep in any culture that they are rarely stated, never questioned, and produce surprise in a person called upon to defend them. They are simply taken as givens which any intelligent, cultured individual anywhere would accept. Needless to say, every intelligent, cultured individual in the world *doesn't* accept all of *our* cultural truths. In fact, many, even most, of the world's people operate on their own cultural truths, which may be 180° at variance with ours.

The following list, initially developed by L. Robert Kohls, draws heavily upon the work of Alfred J. Kraemer of the Human Resources Research Organization (HumRRO).[5] We are also indebted to Francis L. K. Hsu for his work in this field, especially for his excellent comparison of American and Chinese cultural assumptions in *The Study of Literate Civilizations*.[6] *Managing Cultural Differences*[7] by Philip R. Harris and Robert T. Moran also examines the cultural truths of Americans, some of which you may wish to incorporate into the abbreviated list which follows:

- People control their lives and their environments and should reject the idea of fate
- Change is inevitable and desirable
- Equality and egalitarianism are social ideals
- The individual is more important than the group
- Self-help is preferred to dependence
- Competition and free enterprise are best for economic development
- The future is more important than the past
- Action is better than contemplation
- Informality is desirable in social interaction
- Directness and openness are virtues
- The practical is more important to deal with than the abstract, ideal, or intellectual
- Improving material existence benefits human beings more than spiritual improvement
- Problem solving is the best approach to dealing with reality
- Cause-and-effect logic helps us make sense of human existence

3. Give the groups between fifteen and twenty-five minutes to select the cultural truths that apply in their region or subculture and write down examples of them.

4. Have the groups share their lists. Ask everyone to look for what the reports have in common and what appears unique. If there is enough time, everyone can gather around each chart. If time is short or the group is large, have each group appoint a reporter to stay with the chart, and have the rest of each group rotate clockwise around the room at your direction.

> **Note:** Facilitator should be prepared to deal with a situation that may arise from participants confusing a "value" statement with a description of reality—e.g., Americans may "value" equality, yet not put this belief into everyday practice.

---

*Developed by Michael L. G. Berney.

Resource 6B

Cultural Values Contrast*

- Goal: To examine contrasts between American values and those held by other societies.
- Group size: Variable.
- Materials: Flip charts and markers; index cards.
- Advance preparation: See p. 42 for instructions on preparing a set of value cards prior to conducting the exercise. Set up the room so that there will be groups of four people seated in semicircles facing flip charts posted on the wall or on easels around the perimeter of the room. On each flip chart draw a vertical line to divide the chart into two columns. At the top of the left-hand column, write "United States" (or draw an American flag). At the top of the right-hand column, write "Other Country." Write the objective and task on the blackboard or a separate flip chart (and keep covered or hidden):

Objective: To identify value contrasts between the United States and other countries.

Task:

A. Examine the set of values.

B. Sort the set into a group of values that applies in the United States and a group of values that may apply in other countries.

C. Write the values on the chart in a way that will indicate pairs of contrasting values between the United States (left column) and other countries (right column).

Value Cards

- Control over environment
- Change as positive
- Control over time
- Equality/fairness
- Individualism/independence
- Self-help/initiative
- Competition
- Future orientation

- Fate/destiny
- Stability/tradition/continuity
- Close human interaction
- Hierarchy/rank/status
- Group welfare/dependence
- Birthright/inheritance
- Cooperation
- Past orientation

- Action/work orientation
- Informality
- Directness/openness/honesty
- Practicality/efficiency
- Materialism/acquisitiveness

- "Being" orientation
- Formality
- Indirectness/ritual/"face"
- Idealism/theory
- Sprituality/detachment

Procedure

1. Ask participants to look around the room. Each should find one person he or she does not know and walk over and introduce him- or herself to that person. When all are in pairs, ask them again to look around the room, find one other pair they do not know, and walk over and introduce themselves to that pair. Then ask the resulting groups of four to take seats facing one of the flip charts.

2. Prepare sets of value cards by writing each of the above values on a separate card. Distribute a set of value cards to each group.

3. Reveal the Objective/Task flip chart and introduce the purpose and procedure for this exercise. Clarify the task.

4. Give the groups fifteen to twenty minutes to complete the task. Circulate to observe the groups at work. If questions arise (for example, "What do we do if a value does not fit clearly in one column or the other?" or "What does this value statement mean?"), leave it to that group to decide by consensus how to address that problem or question.

5. After the exercise, share and discuss: In relation to other countries, what values do we all consider to be "American values"? What appear to be the greatest areas of conflict or contrast between U.S. values and values in other countries? How will these affect communication between the two cultures?

---

*Contributed by Michael L. G. Berney.

Resource 7

Observations of Foreign Visitors about American Behavior*

- Goal: To increase awareness of how others perceive most Americans.
- Group size: Variable.
- Materials: Index cards, flip charts, pens.
- Advance preparation: Write out quotations (see below) on index cards.

Procedure

1. Divide the group into subgroups of three or four.
2. Hand out different quotations to each subgroup. A larger than necessary number of quotations are presented here so that the facilitator may be selective in choosing the ones which are particularly appealing or appropriate for a specific group.
3. Assignment: Discuss the following questions (put on flip chart):
   a. What is the issue?
   b. Is the criticism true? Fair?
   c. What underlies it? What is the logic behind it?
   d. How could you explain or defend it?
4. Each subgroup reports orally to the whole group.

Quotations of Foreign Visitors†

1. Visitor from India:

   "Americans seem to be in a perpetual hurry. Just watch the way they walk down the street. They never allow themselves the leisure to enjoy life; there are too many things to do."

2. Visitor from Japan:

   "Family life in the U.S. seems harsh and unfeeling compared to the close ties in our country. Americans don't seem to care for their elderly parents."

3. Visitor from Kenya:

   "Americans appear to us rather distant. They are not really as close to other people—even fellow Americans—as Americans overseas tend to portray...."

It's like building a wall. Unless you ask an American a question, he will not even look at you. Individualism is very high."

4. Visitor from Turkey:

"Once...in a rural area in the middle of nowhere, we saw an American come to a stop sign. Though he could see in both directions for miles and no traffic was coming, he still stopped!"

5. Visitor from Colombia:

"The tendency in the U.S. to think that life is only work hits you in the face. Work seems to be the one motivation."

6. Visitor from Indonesia:

"The atmosphere at a sorority party looks very intimate, but if the same people met on the street, they might just ignore one another. Americans look warm, but when a relationship starts to become personal, they try to avoid it."

7. Visitor from Indonesia:

"In the U.S. everything has to be talked about and analyzed. Even the littlest thing has to be 'Why? Why? Why?' I get a headache from such persistent questions. I still can't stand a hard-hitting argument."

8. Visitor from Ethiopia:

"The American seems very explicit; he wants a 'Yes' or 'No'—if someone tries to speak figuratively, the American is confused."

9. Visitor from Ethiopia:

"Trying to establish an interpersonal relationship in the U.S. is like trying to negotiate over or break down a wall; it is almost like a series of concentric circles. You have to break down different levels before you become friends."

10. Visitor from Iran:

"It is puzzling when Americans apply the word 'friend' to acquaintances from almost every sector of one's past or present life, without necessarily implying close ties or inseparable bonds."

11. Visitor from Iran:

"The first time my professor told me: 'I don't know the answer—I will have to look it up,' I was shocked. I asked myself, 'Why is he teaching me?' In my country a professor would give a wrong answer rather than admit ignorance."

12. Visitor from Indonesia:

"The [American] wife of my English professor in Indonesia once asked me why I never invited her to my house. I frankly could not give her a direct answer. There was no reason why I should invite her since there were no parties being held by my family, or if she really wanted to come to the house, she was always welcome at any time. I know now that in America you cannot come freely to anyplace unless you are invited."

13. Visitor from Indonesia:

"The questions Americans ask me are sometimes very embarrassing, like whether I have ever seen a camera. Most of them consider themselves the most highly civilized people. Why? Because they are accustomed to technical inventions. Consequently, they think that people living in bamboo houses or having customs different from theirs are primitive and backward."

14. Visitor from Indonesia:

"I was so surprised and confused when, on leaving Whittier Hall, the provost, in person, held the door for me in order to let me pass before he would enter the door. I was so confused that I could not find the words to express my gratefulness, and I almost fell on my knees as I would certainly do back home. A man who is by far my superior is holding the door for me, a mere student and a nobody."

15. Visitor from Indonesia:

"In America, people show hospitality to strangers, but do not care for family members."

16. Visitor from Hong Kong:

"In my family where I stayed for the weekend, I was surprised to see the servant eating with the children and calling the children by their Christian names."

17. Visitor from Australia:

"I am impressed by the fact that American teachers never seem to stop going to school themselves."

18. Visitor from Vietnam:

"Americans are handy people (even the women). They do almost everything in the house by themselves, from painting walls and doors to putting glass in their windows. Most of them showed me the pretty tables and bookshelves they made by themselves in their spare time."

19. Visitor from Kenya:

"In American schools, the children are restless, inattentive, and rebellious [and the teachers have] poor class discipline."

20. Visitor from Kenya:

"Parents are so occupied earning the weekly or monthly pay that they find very little time to devote to their children."

21. Visitor from Kenya:

"...there is very widespread neglect of respect which children ought to give to adults [in the U.S.]."

22. Visitor from The Philippines:

"They say children everywhere are the same. In my observations I found out a couple of ways where children differ. Children in the United States are very forward in their way of speaking, even to their parents and elders. Children here show a lack of respect for old age. Also, I have observed that children here do not offer their services to their parents willingly. They either have to be told what is to be done or they have to be given some reward or compensation for what they do."

23. Visitor from The Philippines:

"In the United States I have observed that the mother is the dominant parent in most families."

24. Visitor from Algeria:

"I was horrified at the ignorance of the high school students about my country—Algeria. They knew nothing at all about it—location, people, language, political condition. What made it worse was the ignorance of the teacher herself. Her knowledge was very shallow and, in certain instances, quite erroneous."

25. Visitor from Japan:

"Unfortunately, I have been given a bad impression by some American students who speak of their own country very badly, especially of its foreign policy. I knew all the foreign policy of America isn't good, but I did not want to be told so by a native. I hate people who speak badly of their own land, even if they speak the truth."

26. Visitor from Korea:

"In a twelfth-grade social studies class, the teacher gave choices of assignment for the next class. I didn't like the idea of pupils choosing the assignment. I wonder what these pupils will do later in life when there are no choices in the duty assigned to them. They must learn while they are in school how to do well the jobs assigned to them from above."

27. Visitor from Afghanistan:

"I was so much surprised by the many people in America who were under special diet to lose their weight. In our society we are in search of food in order to gain weight."

28. Visitor from Egypt:

"My hostess asked me, 'Would you like to settle down in our country for good?' She was surprised when my answer was in the negative, though I took great pains to make it as diplomatic as possible."

29. Visitor from Taiwan:

"Before I came to America, I always heard how hardworking Americans are, but compared to my people they don't seem to work very hard at all. Why, Americans only work five days a week!"

30. Visitor from Japan:

"The Americans were very kind to invite me into their homes for dinner, but always, as soon as dinner was over, they would ask if I wanted to take a tour of their house as if it was some sort of a monument. I really did not want to, but I could not tell them no, so I said, 'Yes, please.' They were so proud to show off all their prized possessions. It made me think that Americans are all very materialistic. I was also shocked that the bathtub and toilet are always together in an American home and at how close the toilet usually is to the kitchen."

31. Visitor from Guyana:

"The average American male doesn't leave any doubt in your mind that he is unhappy that you (as a foreigner) are here. He doesn't make you feel comfortable."

32. Visitor from Somalia:

"I am worried that you have too much democracy in America. There are so many separate voices and so many selfish interests that you cannot accomplish anything for the general good of the country. You are even prevented from controlling your criminal element for fear of denying the criminal his freedom. That's too much freedom for your own good!"

33. Visitor from The People's Republic of China:

"Why was it necessary to hold a public trial to determine whether John Hinkley was guilty of shooting President Reagan when the very proof of his guilt was captured on television? And then—why was he not executed for such an action? Such leniency only encourages more violence and more law-breaking."

34. Visitor from Lesotho:

"Some Americans I have met seem to like to live with animals, more than with people, and they treat their pets like human beings, even kissing them and holding them on their laps."

35. Visitor from Indonesia:

"I have been offended by how little most Americans know about my country. They either think it is completely underdeveloped or a jungle full of wild animals. Even when I find an American who knows something about Indonesia, it is invariably only the negative things that he knows about, such as a repressive government or the corruption of our officials."

36. Visitor from Cameroon:

"It is shocking to me to see how the father and mother in America kick out of their family their own children when they become eighteen years of age. The most surprising thing about it all is that the young people do not seem to mind it or think it is too cruel to be thrown out of their own family, but they accept it as the natural and normal way of behaving."

37. Visitor from Sudan:

"The hardest thing for me to accept and get used to when I first came to your country was how impersonal and unhuman everything was. Whenever I bought a Coca-Cola or a chocolate bar or a postage stamp I had to buy it from a machine rather than from a living person. You can't talk to a machine, and even when it gives you a candy bar, a machine cannot give you a satisfying relationship. But in your country many people want to spend their time by themselves rather than by talking to other people in a friendly conversation."

38. Visitor from Sweden:

"I have been most negatively impressed by the patronizing attitude of many of the Americans with whom I discussed Third World countries. Some of them were very definite in saying they believed that the people of the Third World were underdeveloped because they were lazy and did not work hard enough."

39. Visitor from Spain:

"It has surprised me most to learn how self-critical many Americans are of their own country and their own people's behaviors. They commonly belittle so many American actions—especially the official actions of their national government. They do not seem to realize that this criticism will reflect negatively on themselves. How can other countries accept the actions and policies of the United States if her own people openly talk against her?"

40. Visitor from Colombia:

"I was surprised, in the United States, to find so many young people who were not living with their parents, although they were not yet married. Also, I was surprised to see so many single people of all ages living alone, eating alone, and walking the streets alone. The United States must be the loneliest country in the world."

41. Visitor from Sweden:

"The difficulty with shopping from the beginning was there was so much to choose among. There were so many brands and the supermarkets were so big!"

42. Visitor from Germany:

"When our little son had a tonsillectomy, he had some complications, needing quite a bit of blood transfusions. I was very much surprised that a blood drive was voluntarily started at the company for him. They hardly knew him, and I was relatively new to the firm. We were really touched by this kind of neighborhood help."

43. Visitor from The Netherlands:

"America is really a salesman's society....They are always selling something. They're selling their product, their company, their services and, last but not least, they are selling themselves—and doing quite well at it too."

44. Visitor from The Netherlands:

"Imagine my astonishment when I went to the supermarket and looked at eggs. You know, there are no small eggs in America; they just don't exist. They tend to be jumbo, extra large, large or medium. It doesn't matter that the medium are little. Small eggs don't exist [in America] because, I guess, they think that might be bad or denigrating."

45. Visitor from Australia:

"When I talk to Americans they never *really* want to disagree. Why are they so afraid to show their colors? They talk like resumes instead of letting you know who they really are. We want blokes who care enough to disagree with us."

---

*Developed by L. Robert Kohls.

†Observations are taken from actual comments made by foreigners about Americans; they are not fabricated.

■ Examples 1 through 17 are quotations collected by John P. Fieg and John G. Blair in *There Is a Difference: Seventeen Intercultural Perspectives.*[8]

■ Examples 18 through 30 are from *American Education through Foreign Eyes*[9] edited by Anthony Scarangello.

■ Examples 31 through 33, and 35 through 42 are from Robert Kohls's research.

■ Example 34 is from Dr. Charles Vetter.

■ Examples 43 and 44 are from the film series *Going International*[10] produced by Griggs Productions, San Francisco, CA.

■ Example 45 is adapted from *A Fair Go for All: Australian/American Interactions*[11] by George W. Renwick and revised by Reginald Smart and Don L. Henderson, published by Intercultural Press, Yarmouth, ME.

Resource 8

Most Common Stereotypes of Americans Held by Foreigners*[12]

- Goal: To increase awareness of how Americans are perceived by foreigners.
- Group size: Variable.

Procedure

1. Have participants brainstorm what stereotypes they think foreigners have of Americans. Examples may be drawn from Resource 7—which will be especially meaningful if the participants have already done that exercise. The following list can be used to help complete the participants' list.

   - outgoing, friendly
   - informal
   - loud, rude, boastful, immature
   - hardworking
   - extravagant, wasteful
   - think they have all the answers
   - not class-conscious
   - disrespectful of authority
   - racially prejudiced
   - know little about other countries
   - all American women are promiscuous
   - wealthy
   - generous
   - always in a hurry
   - disregard for the elderly

This is by no means a complete list. Add other stereotypes you have encountered.

2. Ask the following questions:
   - How many of these stereotypes are true or deserved?
   - How many are positive points?
   - What are the sources of such stereotypes? (American tourists, movies, TV programs, YOU?)

3. It is easy to see why we have been called "Ugly Americans." Even if these stereotypes are untrue, undeserved, or if you personally are not guilty, you will be blamed for them. Additionally, most of the ones that *we* consider positive may be considered negative by foreigners. What examples of this last point can you think of?

---

*Developed by L. Robert Kohls.

Resource 9

Discovering American Values through American Proverbs*

- Goal: To discover American values by analyzing proverbs and discussing which ones hold true today and for whom.
- Group size: Variable.
- Materials: Blackboard or flip chart, pen and paper.

Procedure

1. Write on the blackboard or flip chart:
   - Cleanliness is next to godliness.
   - Time is money.
   - A woman's place is in the home.[13]
   - Little children should be seen and not heard.
2. Ask everyone in the group to take five minutes or so to write down all the American axioms and proverbs they can think of which are most frequently heard.
3. Collect these and then share them by writing them on the left side of the blackboard or flip chart.
4. Then, next to each axiom, determine (as a group) what *value* is being taught.

EXAMPLES	VALUES
Cleanliness is next to godliness	Cleanliness
A penny saved is a penny earned	Thriftiness
Don't cry over spilt milk	Practicality
Waste not; want not	Frugality
Early to bed, early to rise	Diligence
God helps those who help themselves	Initiative
It's not whether you win or lose…	Good sportsmanship
A man's home is his castle	Privacy; private property
You've made your bed; now lie in it	Responsibility; personal choice

These are only a few random examples. The list is long, but the point has been made. With only a dozen or so axioms, you can show clearly how values are embedded in a culture.

> **Note:** Values change and evolve over time. Frugality is not the value it once was in American life, for example. Keep that in mind when discussing values in the context of traditional proverbs.

5. You might want to have the group brainstorm other basic American values that are not on the list, or have them compare the above values with those expressed in the following:

Chinese Editor's Rejection Slip

> We have read your manuscript with boundless delight. If we were to publish your paper, however, it would then be impossible for us to publish any work of a lower standard. And it is unthinkable that in the next thousand years we shall see its equal. We are, to our regret, compelled to return your divine composition and to beg you one thousand times to overlook our short-sighted timidity. (*South China Mail* published in Hong Kong)

---

*Developed by L. Robert Kohls.

Resource 9A

Discovering American Values through American Media*

- Goal: To discover American values by analyzing American heroes or by analyzing advertisements or cartoons.
- Group size: Variable.

Procedure

1. Ask individuals to form small groups of four to five and then to compile a list of favorite heroes or heroines ascertaining their most prominent characteristics and the values they imply. Examples:

   John Wayne—rugged individualism, competition, self-help, directness

   Martin Luther King—action, optimism, future orientation, nonviolence, self-help

   John F. Kennedy—change, self-help

   Harriet Tubman—equality, freedom, self-help, change

   Elizabeth Cady Stanton—equality

   (These are only examples. Make alternative selections as you wish.)

2. Alternatively, give participants advertisements or cartoons from newspapers, magazines, etc. and have them name the values implied in them.

3. Ask groups to share their analyses and compile a common list of American values. These can be printed on flip charts and posted.

---

*Developed by Kay T. C. Clifford.

Resource 9B

Discovering American Values through American Television Series*

- Goal: To explore authority relations between teachers and students through a medium (television) that both reflects and helps mold U.S. values. (This goal is flexible depending on the video scene chosen for the particular training program being conducted.)

- Group size: Five to sixty people. (If a large group, divide into smaller groups for discussion.)

- Materials: Video equipment, pen and paper, flip chart.

- Advance preparation: Activity requires advance preparation of a five-minute video scene and practice with operating video equipment. Tape a segment of a television program that shows a teacher interacting with students, for example, *Head of the Class.* Then review the segment to find a scene no more than five minutes long that exemplifies certain American values, for instance, informality, equality, initiative, directness, openness, egalitarianism, individualism, competition, action orientation, problem-solving orientation, materialism, practicality. (Try other television programs like *The Bill Cosby Show, Roseanne, Perfect Strangers,* or whatever is current.) Prepare a debriefing sheet (with copies for all participants) that introduces the program, in this case *Head of the Class,* and poses questions for discussion following the viewing, such as:
  - What is the relationship between the teacher and the students?
  - What is the teacher trying to teach the students?

Copy the debriefing questions at the top of separate pages of a flip chart, then write at the top of an additional flip chart page the question "Where do people learn their values?" Arrange the flip chart pages so that only the last question is visible as people enter the room.

Procedure

1. Ask the group to name places where people learn values and then record their responses on the visible flip chart page. Their list should include "school" and "media" as well as others. Then explain that in this session the group will view a segment of a television program about a school (or whatever has been

chosen). This will provide a chance to identify some values that are being taught in school, or at least portrayed on television.

2. Distribute the debriefing sheet, and ask everyone to read it and consider the questions while watching the videotape.

3. Show the videotape.

4. Ask everyone to take five minutes to write down responses to the questions on the debriefing sheet.

5. Then collect responses and write them on the flip chart pages that you have prepared.

6. Ask the group to review with you the responses you have collected, and try to summarize what basic American values are present in the scene they have viewed. Circle or add these to the charts.

You might want to return to the list of places, recorded on the first flip chart page, where people said they learned their values and ask the group how they might go about studying values being taught in other settings.

---

*Developed by Michael L. G. Berney.

Resource 10

Communication and Intercultural Interactions[*14]

- Goal: To show the impact of communication on cross-cultural interactions.
- Group size: Variable.
- Materials: Flip chart.

Procedure

Present the following material as a lecturette.

What is Communication?

According to Pierre Casse in his book *Training for the Cross-Cultural Mind,* communication is a "...process by which two individuals 'try' to exchange a set of ideas, feelings, symbols...meanings."

Intercultural communication is a "...process by which two individuals who do not belong to the same culture 'try' to exchange a set of ideas, feelings, symbols...meanings." Since they do not belong to the same culture, it "implies that they do not share the same assumptions, beliefs, values or...same ways of thinking, feeling, and behaving. This phenomenon makes the communication process much more difficult and challenging than we think."

In addition, Casse emphasizes the following five facts about communication that have an impact on all cross-cultural exchanges.

Present the following statements, and initiate a group discussion of each.

1. Pure communication is impossible, as we all bring prior associations to the communication process.

   Ask participants to free-associate when you say the word "car," for example. Since meaning is in people and not in words, you will get a variety of answers. Explore factors that might affect communication, such as emotional connotations and "semantic environments." For example, how does communication differ in a church as compared to a locker room?

2. We communicate in many ways, and much of our communication is unconscious.

   Ask participants to interlock their fingers and observe which thumb is on top. Then have them switch the position of their thumbs and be aware of their discomfort. (Point to be made: much of our communication is unconscious, and we don't realize how natural it is until we are in a situation where it isn't natural.) Ask participants to analyze how we dress, use time and space, and touch one another.

3. We see what we expect to see. (In other words, we provide meaning to life.)

   In order to make sense of the world, we use a "cultural map" in our minds which often leads us astray. Our preconceived definitions impede us from dealing creatively with reality. On a flip chart or blackboard draw a swastika, with the right-angle extensions bent in a counterclockwise direction, and ask the participants what they see. How many of them identify it as a Nazi rather than Navajo, Buddhist, Indian, or Persian symbol? In the Nazi symbol the right-angle extensions bend clockwise.

   Navajo =   Nazi =

   Of further interest is that, according to the second edition of *Webster's New Twentieth-Century Dictionary*, the word "swastika" comes from the Sanskrit *svasti* meaning well-being or benediction.

4. We don't see what we don't expect to see.

   △ ONCE IN A A LIFETIME   △ PARIS IN THE THE SPRING   △ BIRD IN THE THE HAND

   Write the preceding sayings in three equilateral triangles on a flip chart. Allow the participants to read them quickly; then, after covering up the chart, ask them to recite the sayings. Few people will see the double article in each saying. What we see is dependent upon what we want to see, what our training has been, what makes sense, and what fits our cognitive map.

5. We all perceive things differently.

   This is the typical situation of witnesses at an accident giving the police different descriptions of what happened. Using the "Ambiguous Lady" (which alternately takes the shape of a young woman and an old woman), let the participants argue about which it is. (See *Survival Kit for Overseas Living*, p. 58—citation in Appendix C.)

In summary, *we* create the reality upon which our communication is based. We bring prior assumptions and associations, many of which are culturally based, to the process of communication. We can never assume that the assumptions we operate under are the same for everyone, particularly when we are engaged in cross-cultural communication.[15]

---

*Adapted from Pierre Casse by John M. Knight.

Resource 11

Martian Anthropology Exercise*16

- Goal: To give the participants an opportunity to gain a different perspective on American culture.
- Group size: Variable.
- Materials: Notepad and pen/pencil.
- Advance preparation: Participants should have read, before the session, the well-known article "Body Ritual among the Nacirema," by Horace Miner[17] (see Appendix C).

This exercise is offered as an example of the kind of orientation activity which (1) can be developed by any trainer anywhere, (2) can be staged in any setting, making use of locally available resources, situations, and some imagination, and (3) places participants into an active process that requires them to examine their ways of observing while trying out new methods. This exercise was developed by the authors as a modified "drop-off" exercise (a kind of activity in which trainees are dropped off in an unfamiliar community for a day or so and are asked to find out certain kinds of information); it can be done in an hour and a half to two hours. It is also fun. It places the participant in the position of being a stranger or an outsider looking at familiar things from a different point of view. The assignments outlined may be used as models; you will probably need to select assignments appropriate to and available in your situation. The exercise is not limited to the usual sites where orientation workshops take place. It can also be used at professional and other kinds of conferences which take place at large hotels where participant teams can be sent to places such as the hotel beauty parlor, barber-shop, bar, newsstand, gift shop, lobby, parking garage, kitchen, maid's supply center, or simply be assigned to ride an elevator for a half hour or so.

Procedure

1. Organize group members into teams of two, three, or four people. Explain briefly that they are teams of anthropologists from Mars, coming to this strange new culture, Earth, to examine various aspects of the way of life here and how the society functions. A high-level delegation from Mars is planning a state visit to Earth in the near future. The Martian rulers want to understand the important elements of life on earth prior to the trip, and the anthropologists are being sent as advance research teams, with the assigned task of collecting information. Stress that participants should refer to the Miner article as a model for their observations on American culture.

2. Assignments are then given to each of the teams. The following list will provide an idea of the kinds of assignments which work well. Anecdotes are included with some items to give the reader an indication of the kinds of research findings to expect. The list is by no means exhaustive, but it may suggest excellent alternatives in one's own locale.

- One team was recently sent to McDonald's for an hour to study family life. In addition to observing family roles, child-rearing and other phenomena, the team members introduced themselves as Martian anthropologists and interviewed several of the patrons and workers with good results.

- Another team, sent to a large bowling alley to study religion, immediately recognized the importance of the ten white icons at the end of each long aisle and reported with considerable detail on the significance of the large spheres offered to the gods by the faithful and the forms of physical and religious fervor displayed by the worshipers during the ceremony.

- A third group was sent to a downtown bank to study the education system. They noted that lessons were handled quickly by the educational institutions; an exam was swiftly filled out by the student, a brief report was handed to the teacher, who processed the exam or lesson through a machine and provided the student with paper vouchers in return. These vouchers, it has been noted, can later be exchanged for goods and services within the community, leading the Martians to the interpretation that there is a direct relationship between educational excellence and the society at large. Successful students are rewarded by the society in concrete terms.

- Another team was sent to a supermarket to study agriculture and food gathering. The researchers were puzzled to find fresh fruits and vegetables growing in the absence of organic soil and couldn't understand why the foods seemed to be covered by an invisible shield. They deduced that the contents of food containers could be determined by the pictures on the outside of the containers, although this theory presented problems when the anthropologists passed along an aisle where baby foods or pet foods were displayed.

- A fifth team (age was a factor here) was sent to a workingmen's bar to study politics and government. They noted the importance of the clear golden liquid used by the politicians in solving public problems, and were impressed by the apparent fatigue of the rulers as they entered and their feeling of goodwill, well-being, and political accomplishment when they left an hour later.

- ■ The following is a list of other possible places and research tasks:

  Bookstore to study health and medicine

  Laundromat to study science and technology

  Local ski area to observe military preparedness and defense

  Public library to study kinship networks

  Large discount store—recreation and leisure-time activity

  Paint and wallpaper store to look for art forms, fine arts, cultural expression

  Music shop to explore economy and business

  Local gymnasium, recreation center, health club to study social organization

  Hardware store or factory to explore law and justice

  Bus station to study philosophical thought

3. Pass out the assignments to each team on a slip of paper and dispatch them to complete their research tasks. They should take notepads and pens or pencils to record findings. Give them an hour or an hour and a half, depending on the time you have available. Their task is to bring their research findings back to present them to a panel of Martian scholars.

4. Return to the orientation site. Give the teams enough time to assemble their data (over lunch or during the dinner hour) and then reconvene. Give each team about five minutes to report to the other groups in a large session. Members of other teams are free to comment and ask questions. All reports should be couched in terms parallel to the style used in Miner's Nacirema article.

5. After the five-minute reports there are several options. Here are two.

   a. Members of different research teams can be organized into work groups which are assigned the task of preparing a concise briefing paper about the most important aspects of life on Earth, based on what they have seen. The topics to be included in the briefing paper may include the following (and/or any others you devise):

      - ■ Hierarchical structure or system
      - ■ Communication
      - ■ Travel tips for the VIP Martian delegation: what gifts to bring, proper etiquette, etc.
      - ■ How time is used
      - ■ Beliefs and ideals
      - ■ Customs

- Values
- Private and public behaviors

After presenting their briefing paper(s), discuss how participants developed guidelines for functioning in the target culture and reached the conclusions they did about it. Further discussion might explore applying this "anthropological inquiry" in another culture and what might influence the "anthropologists'" information gathering about and analysis of that culture.

b. The experience gained from the role play, including the reports, can be further explored by having the participants discuss any or all of the following subjects (the facilitator will probably be able to add more):

- The sensation of being strangers, of being outside of and detached from what they were studying and/or of being stared at or otherwise being isolated.

- Their inner feelings before they began and during the exercise, especially as they can be related to feelings they are likely to experience overseas.

- The comparison of our usual ways of seeing things (passive, inattentive, bored, taking things for granted) with the Martian way (intense concentration on all features of the locale, attention to detail, etc.), and the relevance of this to the field-learning situation overseas in terms of observation skills needed, best ways to approach people and institutions, etc.

- The ways in which one can transfer this kind of detailed observation skill (without the game element) to observation and information gathering in the host country to which one goes as a sojourner.

This exercise moves along swiftly, and, as is the case with most exercises, it is very important to debrief the participants in structured discussion afterwards. The exercise is especially valuable in providing participants with a shared experience which draws them together and opens new avenues of learning. It can also be used to break participants out of overly theoretical discussions and to impress upon them the need for initiative and special kinds of skills when they are called upon to try something different. It helps them to detach themselves from their usual behaviors and mindsets and to stand back and gain a different perspective.

---

*Developed by Donald Batchelder and Bill Harshbarger.

Resource 12

Cross-Cultural Journal*

- Goal: To introduce participants to a learning tool they can use in cross-cultural settings to help them analyze why they react as they do to the new culture.
- Group size: Variable.
- Materials: A notebook, similar to a stenographer's notebook, in which pages are divided vertically in right and left halves.

Procedure

On the left side, participants should describe what they observe as they experience the new environment; on the right, they will record their reactions to what they see and try to analyze their observations from a cross-cultural perspective. Depending on the situation, participants could analyze a foreign culture or write an entry based on their encounter with American culture in the Martian Anthropology Exercise. While this is valuable as a self-contained, privately done exercise, it can also provide data for discussions with a "cultural informant," someone from the host culture with the ability to interpret his or her own cultural behavior and values. The following is a sample illustrating how the journal should be set up.

Date:

Location:

OBSERVATION/DESCRIPTION

On this side of the journal, describe what you saw.

Anything that strikes you as different, funny, weird, sad, etc. is appropriate. Feelings, emotions, judgments should not be expressed on this side. Just stick to the facts.

OPINION/ANALYSIS

On this side of the journal, describe your thoughts, feelings, etc. about the event. Then try to analyze why you feel this way. What in your cultural makeup may be affecting how you feel? How is that different from whatever values or assumptions may be at work in the new culture?

The following is a sample drawn from the Martian Anthropology Exercise (Resource 11).

Date: January 5

Location: Commerce Bank

OBSERVATION/DESCRIPTION

People enter the bank and fill out forms. They hand these to a person behind a counter, who processes them and provides paper vouchers, which are later used in exchange for goods and services in the community.

OPINION/ANALYSIS

The bank is this society's educational institution. The people are students, and the forms they fill out constitute exams or reports, which are passed along to the teacher. There is a direct relationship in this society between educational excellence and society at large; students are rewarded immediately and in a very concrete fashion.

The following is an unedited journal entry from a Japanese student analyzing American culture.

Date: Sept. 9

Location: At my host family's house

OBSERVATION/DESCRIPTION

This morning I had to go to school at 8:10, but I could not hear my alarm clock ringing at 6:40, so I overslept until 8:00. My host mother did not wake me up though she heard the alarm clock's sound.

OPINION/ANALYSIS

She was very unkind to me. Maybe she doesn't care if I have many difficulties at school. I felt loneliness. In Japan, people help each other. We always take care of our families and always take care of our friends even if they are grown-up persons. To take care of each other is a most important value for us. Host mother said in the evening, "Next time if you don't wake up, what should I do? I respected your privacy this morning." Her words were very impressive to me. I understood her attitude represented the important American values: individualism and privacy. Maybe she also wanted me to learn "self-help" and "time control" to survive in America.

The following unedited journal entry is from a Chinese international student.

Date: Sept. 1

Location: classroom

OBSERVATION/DESCRIPTION

Some American students prop their feet on the chairs or desks and eat and drink when they are in class.

OPINION/ANALYSIS

I am uncomfortable to see American students' liberal behavior in class. In class, they do as they do at home. In China, every student tries to sit still, keep feet on the floor, no food or drink while in class. Because fathers and teachers taught us to behave. If you brought your breakfast to eat in class, the teacher would point to you coldly and say, "Please don't eat; otherwise, you interfere with other students." Even once one classmate was late for surgery class in my Chinese Med. School. He was pushed out of the classroom as soon as he stepped into the room. It is no way to break the classroom manner. Coming from China, I was amazed to see what American students do. They are less controlled. They do what they enjoy. Maybe they consider it to be freedom. They thought they come to school for knowledge, not restrictions. Whether you achieve in class or not has nothing to do with class conduct. That is the way they live—individual freedom under no restrictions.

*Developed by John M. Knight.

Resource 13

Reflective Mirror Exercise*

- Goal: To elicit awareness of the necessity for careful observation. (This is a good way to close a workshop in which people have had to work together closely and have developed rapport. It also emphasizes the importance of developing the learning skills needed for effective cross-cultural interaction.)
- Group size: Six to sixty people (works best with twenty to thirty).
- Materials: Cassette tape recorder and some mellow, flowing music, such as Pachelbel's "Canon in D," or New Age music like Kitaro's "Silk Road Trilogy" or Andreas Vollenweider's "Behind the Gardens."

Procedure

1. Instruct the participants to follow the instructions below during the exercise.

   Participants should form two parallel lines facing each other with about six to eight feet between the lines. (See diagram on next page.) Depending on the number of people and the size of the room, several pairs of lines may have to be formed. The facilitator instructs one person (P1) at the end of one line (LA) to begin moving in place when the music starts. The person (P2) opposite P1 in the second line (LB) begins to mirror the movement of P1. The person (P3) next to P1 in LA watches P2 in LB and mirrors that movement. This continues down both lines until everyone is sure of whom to mirror. Then the facilitator tells P1 to continue to move with the music with the other people following their "mirrors" until those mirrors stop. When the music stops, P1 should stop and stand still until the last movement has flowed to the end of the line.

2. In the debriefing, the facilitator can ask the participants to describe what happened as they tried to "mirror," how they felt about the experience, and what they think this exercise has to do with cross-cultural interaction. Past participants have commented that they felt foolish, uncomfortable, and awkward during the exercise—feelings that people have when learning to deal with other cultures. They have also said that just the simple task of mirroring an action is not as easy as it seems. Mirroring the actions of another person, becoming aware of the nonverbal communication of another culture, or recording a nonjudgmental observation (see Resource 12) are all equally challenging endeavors. As with the exercise in Resource 1 (Push/Pull), this exercise may not be appropriate for certain audiences. It is up to the facilitator

to decide how much ambiguity and intense nonverbal interaction a particular group of participants can handle.

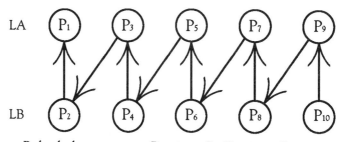

P1 leads the movement; P2 mirrors P1; P3 mirrors P2, etc.

---

*Contributed by John M. Knight.

Resource 14

Simulation Exercise 1—Cultural Encounter*[18]

- Goals: To identify communication cues in an unfamiliar culture, to use systematic information-gathering and analysis techniques, and to explore ambiguities and examine salient factors in cross-cultural interaction from the perspectives of both the host culture and visiting anthropologists.
- Group size: Twelve to sixty people; takes one to two hours.

Procedure

1. Form culture groups of ten to twelve participants and select two anthropologists, one male and one female, per culture. (Volunteers work best.) Having both a male and a female is important but not stressed when asking for volunteers.

   Note: For same-gender groups use any visible category, e.g., differences in hair or eye color, age, etc.; the cultures can also be called "organizations" or "agencies" if that is considered more useful in a business setting.

2. The anthropologists are separated from the culture so that both can receive their instructions.
   - Anthropologists' Instructions:
     a. Interview as many persons of the host culture as possible.
     b. Use research methods—ask several people the same question(s) and verify responses for consistency; observe behavior; look for patterns.
     c. After ten minutes you will be asked to describe the culture. Anthropologist "interview guides" have been developed and are used by some trainers. (See "The Anthropologist Interview Guide," p. 76.)
   - Host Cultures' Instructions:
     a. Men can only talk with men and women can only talk with women. (In same-gender groups, blondes can only talk with blondes, or blue eyes with blue eyes, or older people with older people—depending upon the categorizing principle you use.)
     b. You can only answer yes or no questions.
     c. If the anthropologist is smiling when the question is asked, the answer is "yes"; if the anthropologist is not smiling, the answer is "no."

3. Interaction:
   a. Allow the teams of anthropologists to confer briefly among themselves, then introduce them to the cultures.
   b. Encourage them to talk with as many people as possible.
   c. If the anthropologists ask if they can talk with each other, the preferred answer is that it's up to them. If you have set this up with a group of anthropologists responsible for interviewing the whole culture, they obviously can ask questions of anyone. However, if you have organized the group into smaller cultures with "assigned" anthropologists, the anthropologists may ask if they could interview people in other cultures. The preferred response is again that it's up to them. The interaction period should last approximately ten minutes.

Debriefing

Description Phase:

Ask the anthropologists to describe the cultures (or their problems).

Then ask them if the people in the culture were happy and consistent in their replies to questions.

Next, ask people from the host culture to describe their rules, so that the anthropologists are no longer in the dark, and then to describe their experience. Be careful to protect the dignity and self-image of the anthropologists, as it is easy for them to feel that they have been made to look foolish.

Analysis Phase:

Ask such questions as:

- What is the process by which misunderstanding occurs?
- Why does it result in frustration for both anthropologist and host culture?
- What is the anthropologist's role in affecting the response of those in the host culture?
- Explore the process by which we develop elaborate explanations for interpersonal dynamics, e.g., experts rarely look at themselves, but blame those they are observing for being "dumb," "uncooperative," or "inconsistent."
- What real-world cultures and personal experiences does this exercise remind you of?

Generalization Phase:

Ask what people learned as a result of this exercise. Each group will generate its own learning, depending on the play of the exercise, the training agenda, the intended use of the results, etc. But you should be prepared with a few things that you want to emphasize or introduce (if they aren't brought up in the group). Some of these points might be:

- Being systematic yields more information.
- The information we gather is often a projection of ourselves.
- Stress was produced in the cultures because the instructions to the participants called on them to display "impolite" behavior; cultural rules were forced on them.
- No one really explains all the rules in a new culture so there's a lot of pressure on outside experts or anyone else attempting to function within it.
- Attributions are culturally based.
- Confusion and inconsistent data are often signals that there is an underlying cultural clash.
- Being seen as a person who answers questions readily is often equated with being a cultural leader, but it's only a perception.

Application Phase:

Ask the participants how they will use what they learned in this exercise.

An interview guide for the anthropologists follows. You may wish to adapt it for your own workshop. Questions nine to thirteen should be formulated by the anthropologists.

The Anthropologist Interview Guide

You are on an information-gathering mission to a foreign culture. You will ask as many individuals as possible the yes/no questions listed below; tabulate your responses and present the conclusions to members of the society. After asking the questions on the interview guide, you may continue by generating at least five additional specific yes/no questions on the problem and/or solution. Be sure to interview at least two people for each question. You will have ten minutes to complete the collection of data.

1. Are all of you from the same culture?
2. Do all of you speak the same language?
3. Are you friendly to outsiders?
4. Do you practice the same religion?
5. Is the same food prepared by all culture members?
6. Do you live in extended families?
7. Are children educated in public schools?
8. Are most people in cities?

Please add your own questions:

9.

10.

11.

12.

13.

Questions for the anthropologist:

1. To what extent is the group friendly and cooperative?
2. To what extent is the group reasonable and consistent in their thinking?

---

*Adapted from Paul Pedersen by Sandra Mumford Fowler.

Resource 15

Simulation Exercise 2—Minoria-Majoria Simulation*

- Goal: To help Americans experience the feelings associated with the donor-recipient relationships which exist in many intercultural transactions.
- Group size: Fifteen to sixty. Takes two to three hours to play and debrief.
- Materials:

MINORIANS	MAJORIANS
(given only minimal supplies)	(given luxurious materials)
Newsprint (or old newspapers)	Colored crepe paper
Brass fasteners	Colored tissue paper
String	Paper doilies
	Scotch tape
	Masking tape
	Scissors
	Other similar materials

Procedure

1. Divide the participants into two groups.
2. Have both groups make arm bands which they will wear throughout the exercise. Minorians wear black crepe paper arm bands for identification; Majorians wear white crepe paper arm bands.
3. Give each group *separate* briefings (see scenarios below). You will need two rooms and two facilitators for this initial briefing. Don't let the groups hear each other's scenario until the debriefing following the simulation.

Instructions to Minorians

You are residents of the country of Minoria. Minoria is not a new country, but a very old one with a noble history and a rich culture. Unfortunately, your country has been dominated by other nations for so long that you are just now beginning to regain a sense of independence and pride. You have finally been able to shake yourself free of the nations which have dominated and exploited you for so long, and you are very jealous of your hard-won freedom and your right to run your country the way you want to.

One of the problems that besets you is the fact that you have few natural resources and, because you have been dominated by others for so long, you have not been able to develop the resources you have or the technology to make use of them. Poverty is a problem in your country, but it is one you have learned to live with and even to accept as the normal way of life.

This is the anniversary of your independence, and you are searching for some appropriate monument, symbol, or other manifestation around which the new national pride can form and develop. Your task is to begin discussing what kind of monument will best symbolize that pride and then to construct it with the materials and resources you have at hand. You want to use native materials to the extent possible, partly out of the very pride you are celebrating. Additionally, you do not have the money to import materials, and you do not want to become indebted to outsiders. You are especially wary of gifts with political strings attached.

You have just received word from the ministry that in the next twenty minutes a team of people will be arriving from a country called Majoria. Although you have never had an opportunity to meet any Majorians, Majoria is well known to you since it is one of the leading countries in the world. Its resources seem to be endless. While you would welcome suggestions and appreciate any help the Majorians might offer, you are ready to resist any type of patronizing or threat to your independence of choice or action.

After twenty minutes of planning with the *Majorians*, you will have no more than thirty minutes working together to execute the plans you have jointly made. On with your monument! Long live Minoria!

Instructions to Majorians

You are the fortunate citizens of Majoria. Majoria's technology, natural resources, and wealth make it a country without peer in the modern world. Your people have solved the scourges of earlier centuries: epidemics, hunger, limited production, illiteracy, etc. People in your country worry little about survival and more about exploiting their opportunities in a land of abundance.

Unfortunately, there are other far less fortunate countries. Many people in your country are concerned about their plight: some feel guilt for having so much while others have so little; others realize that the world will not long be safe if the imbalance of technology, resources, and materials continues. Because of your idealism and your genuine concern for less fortunate people, you have volunteered to go to an obscure little country named Minoria and offer aid. Minoria is a poor, underdeveloped nation, but within it, side by side, there are dramatic contrasts: affluence and need, healthy, handsome leaders and starving beggars, modern buildings and shacks without sanitation, educated urbanites and the illiterate country people. Behind Minoria's plush front, the statistics of hunger, disease, and unemployment tell the real story. Minoria is new among the world's nations and its leaders, policymakers and technicians are inexperienced at their work. Frequently things are done on the merest whim and have no relation to the country's basic needs or long-term interests.

Minoria needs many things. It is struggling to survive in the modern world. Many fear it will not. Most important for Minoria is to order its priorities to place the few resources it has where the greatest needs lie. Next, it must acquire resources from outside to supplement its own. Finally, technical help is needed to make sure what they construct endures and what they have or are provided with is used well.

You have ten minutes to discuss what you will do to assist Minoria before arriving in the country. (**Note to trainer:** This discrepancy with the "twenty minutes" indicated in "Instructions to Minorians" is intentional. The Majorians are to arrive ten minutes before the Minorians expect them.) After your arrival, you will be expected to help them plan a major, top priority project that will benefit their country and to help execute that plan using the materials you have at hand.

Remember, you will be evaluated on your ability to:

a. Help them reset priorities which match their needs,

b. Help them use the materials you have brought wisely,

c. Provide technical assistance and helpful suggestions about the construction of the selected project.

Discussion

After the simulation, debrief the participants and discuss the experience with them while they are still in their roles and still wearing their arm bands so they can discuss the experience from their "cultural" viewpoint. The initial discussion can focus on how the participants feel the simulation relates to the purpose of the workshop or training session. Some points which need to be emphasized are that the Minorians must be able to maintain pride in their accomplishments even though they may need technical assistance and that it is not easy for a person or society that is poor to receive aid gracefully, especially if it is given on someone else's terms. It is important that these points become clear to both groups by the end of the discussion.

On the other hand, the Majorians may feel rejected and not appreciated since they came with a genuine interest in helping. They may also feel that they have a right to see that the material they have brought is properly used and not wasted. In the end, each side needs to develop an understanding of how the other feels about the project, since this simulation is basically an exercise in how to view a problem or a situation from a totally different point of view. The facilitator may want to point out that this skill, i.e., viewing things from the perspective of another group or culture, has domestic as well as international application, e.g., homelessness in the U.S. In addition to these ideas for general discussion, the facilitator may also pursue some of the following specific questions:

- How easy was it for you to take on your role in the simulation?
- What were your reactions when you entered the other culture?
- What did you think when the experts arrived in your culture, especially since they came earlier than expected?
- Did the participants in the other group react as you had anticipated they would?
- What were your expectations for yourself and your culture? What were your expectations of the other culture?
- How did you feel at different stages during the simulation?

Finally, there is a "derobing ceremony." All participants rip off their arm bands and throw them into a common wastebasket. (Moving participants out of the roles they have played is essential to end any resentment or hostility which may have developed from the simulation.) After the derobing ceremony, ask the participants how it feels to step out of their roles and view the exercise from another perspective.

---

*Developed by Tad Erlich, L. Robert Kohls, Margo Kiely, and Bill Hoffman.

Resource 16

Case Studies[19]

Case studies provide another way of looking at intercultural interactions. Since we are not immediately involved in the situation presented, we have the opportunity to explore objectively what happened, why it happened, and how it might have been prevented. Some of the cases which follow in this resource simply describe the event; others take the format of a cultural assimilator, presenting a critical incident and asking the reader to choose the most appropriate action to take in response to the incident. Some cases provide useful cultural background, some do not. Whichever kind of exercise it is, remember that there may not be a wholly satisfactory response or acceptable solution.

In analyzing case studies, the following questions can be used as a guide:

- What happened? Answer this from the perspective of as many of the parties involved as possible.
- What is the situation or problem? Again, answer from the perspective of the people involved. How does it involve values, language, nonverbals?
- How are the individuals in the case study related? Peers, guest-host?
- How can the situation be resolved? Consider as many courses of action as possible.
- What are the probable results (or repercussions) of each "solution"? Are the solutions at one extreme or the other, or is a compromise possible? Is a solution even possible? If there is no solution, how do Americans, who generally feel that problems must have solutions, deal with it?
- Is additional information needed to make a decision?
- Consider the issues involved in light of this quote from T. E. Lawrence (of Arabia):

    How could I, as me, meet these new people?

    How would I have to change?

    What of me was superficial and might be sacrificed, and what need I keep to remain myself?

This clearly illustrates the dilemma that we, as Americans, encounter in interaction with people from other cultures. Can we change to fit the new situation instead of always expecting others to adapt to us?

Note: Even if the content of the case study or critical incident seems dated and even though it may involve participants in occupations not related to those in the training group, the differences in values and modes of intercultural communication are still valid topics of inquiry. Also, we reiterate that there are no single right solutions to many complex situations and no easy answers. In fact, there may be no solutions at all to some problems. The important thing is that it helps people come to the awareness that there is more than one possible valid point of view on an issue because very different value systems are involved. Like everything else, case studies are imperfect. In some incidents, for example, the characters may look like stereotypes. How will the facilitator deal with this if the participants point it out? How does it reflect the perception of the author of the case study and/or the perception of the participants in the workshop? For the skilled facilitator, deficiencies in the case studies become opportunities to enhance the learning.

The reader will note that many of the case studies come from two sources: The Bridges of Understanding series by V. Lynn Tyler (originals are in the Brigham Young University David M. Kennedy Center for International Studies) and the Peace Corps.[20] They constitute only the tip of the iceberg as far as the number of case studies available in the literature. Many, many more excellent cases are available from these and other sources. Several useful short cases may be found in some Resources for Area Studies.[21] (See also "Area Studies Resources," p.138.)

The facilitator might also consider preparing a video case study by selecting a segment of no more than ten minutes from a film or video listed in Appendix B or taping an enactment of a situation he or she constructs. It is helpful to use the case studies provided below as models of the conflicting values which exist in a situation. (See Resource 9B for an example of how to construct a video case study.)

CASE STUDIES

1

Country: Afghanistan

Issue: Efficiency versus Tradition

Source: *Discussion Leader's Manual for Cross-Cultural Studies Training: Afghanistan.* Prepared by Rosalind Pearson and Janet Bing, Peace Corps.

From the Peace Corps Volunteer's Viewpoint

My seventh-grade class had no books. Nearly every day at various times for eight weeks I went to the storeroom where the supply of books was kept. Each time I was told that the keeper was out and that no one else, not even the principal, had the key. I gradually began to visualize this "keeper of the keys" as a mythic man of giant proportions. But, one day, he actually appeared at the storeroom—a wrinkled little man in a gray turban.

I told him that I needed 120 American English Language Book Ones for my seventh-grade classes. I could see the books piled in neat but dusty stacks on the shelves. He looked at me in a puzzled way. "Where are your books?" he asked. Thinking that he had not understood me, I said, "No, you don't understand. I do not have books. That is why I am here. I need to get books for my three seventh-grade classes. I need 120 books."

"No, no," he said, standing firmly in the doorway. "I cannot give you books. I am responsible for the books in this room. I am a very honest man. If I give you the books then I won't have any books, and how will I explain an empty storeroom that was given to me full of books?"

I tried to be patient with the old man. But I had to make him understand the necessity of my getting books.

I had worked orally with my students all this time, but each day they asked me, "Where are our books, *maalem sayb?*" They were eager to have them, particularly since all the upper classes had books. I had tried various ways of writing out exercises for Book One as I had remembered them, but the school had no duplicating machine, and this meant writing out 120 papers by hand.

The government was most anxious to start to distribute the textbooks all over the country in an attempt to standardize the English classes. The Peace Corps was a vital part of this effort. It was even harder to accept the fact that because I was unable to get books for my classes, I was going against the goals set by the Peace Corps and the ministry.

When my kids went on to the eighth grade, they would be poorly prepared indeed if they had never worked with an American English Language text, never learned to read from a printed page (students have a hard time making the jump from handprinted to typed words).

I was responsible for teaching these boys and I owed them my best efforts. What would I have given them if, at the end of the year, they didn't know how to read and they were unprepared for the work of the next grade?

The most frustrating part of all this was that the books were there in the very same building as my students. The books were sitting in the storeroom waiting to be used, and my students were sitting in the classroom waiting to use them. All that stood between the books and the students was a locked door and an illiterate old man with the key to open it.

The keeper was unable to accept my reasoning, was unmoved by my pleading, and when I told him I would take all the responsibility for the books and promised that every book would be back in place at the end of the year, he merely laughed as if he thought I were mad. He could never understand that not using the books was the same as not having them.

I went to the principal to see if he could intervene on my behalf, but there was nothing he could do since he had no key, and the inspector from the ministry would probably not come for several months.

Time was passing, and I was getting more and more desperate. I talked and talked to the keeper, but he remained invincible.

We could have had a thousand Peace Corps Volunteer (PCV) teachers in this country, but if a keeper-of-the-books was behind each of them, nothing would be accomplished. I don't see how this country is going to progress if everything is kept locked up to mold. It's enough to make you give up and go home. I finally wrote to the Peace Corps office. Maybe they could do something about this.

From the Keeper's Viewpoint

It is not every day that an old man like me has the honor of being appointed to a government job. The people of my village are very poor, and we have much difficulty in our lives. I will do this job well, and the government will, perhaps, look with favor upon my son. Our people are used to hardship. My many years of life have seen many evils and have given me some knowledge of the ways of men. If it be the will of Allah, I shall do my work well and bring honor to my family.

Truly it is a great responsibility for me to be entrusted with the room of many fine books. I have not seen such books before in my life. Even though I must travel a great distance from my village to the school, I am proud to do so. Certainly, this school is a very fine school to have so many books.

There is the man named Nasratulian, from the Ministry of Education in the capital city, who comes to the school during the year to look at the storeroom. He is an important man with a high position, and it is my great honor to please him. Should he take a good report of my work to the ministry, it will be very fortunate for my son, my family, and my people. It is great pleasure for me to see in my lifetime such things come to pass, Allah be praised!

There are some things in my work that, with my humble background, are difficult for me to understand. How can I explain to the young and impatient man from America about my position? He has very strange ideas. He does not understand that these boys will lose the books. They are well-meaning boys, but they are mischievous. When the inspector comes to see the books and finds that the books are not here, I will have to pay for them, and how am I to do that? What shame it would be for my family! What should Nasratulian Khan think of me when he finds that some of these valuable books are lost?

And what should he think if he comes to see his humble friend, Kurban Ali, and finds instead the young man from America sitting by the storeroom with the key?

He would think, "Oh, that old man has gone back to the mountain. These people are not suited for such work, as I had suspected all along." That would indeed be a terrible thing. I would disgrace my family; my son would have to be content to farm; his children would be unhappy. No, such a thing will not occur. By the guidance of Allah, I am a good and honest man, and I will live up to the responsibility given to me.

I do not understand what that young man says about his students. I know his students, and they are very content with him. He is indeed a strange person. Imagine, a man from America becoming a Keeper-of-Books! That is truly a strange idea. He seems unhappy here—such a village must be difficult for him. In America, villages are very large. Perhaps his unhappiness makes him discontent with our people.

He does not understand that my responsibility is to make sure that nothing happens to these books. He wants me to have an empty storeroom! What should I do if I had no books to look after? Each time I come, I count the books, and make sure they are neatly stacked. Each time all the books have been counted, and I have not lost one book. This is my responsibility. How can a baker make bread with no flour?

From the Inspector's Viewpoint

It is very difficult to deal with these people who keep our storerooms. They have little understanding, no education, and cannot be trusted. One must be very firm with them, or else there would be all kinds of dishonesty and corruption. It is my responsibility to see that such corruption does not occur. I have forty villages to inspect throughout this province—indeed, a great responsibility.

I must keep my eye on old Kurban Ali—he is the newest storekeeper in the district and, as they say, a new servant can catch a running deer, but he is only of a low caste and his family is poor. These people must be watched because we cannot expect very much from them. He could make a lot of extra money by selling the books.

Also, many new supplies were sent to that school, and it is necessary to make sure that they do not get misplaced. The ministry has been able to increase the production of textbooks, much to the benefit of our country, and we must see that every school in the entire province has the new English books.

I am very careful to keep records of what has been given to the schools in my district. At the beginning of the year, we supplied a total of 1,300 books to the schools. Each time I go to a school, I must make sure that none of the books has been misplaced. The people in the smaller villages are ignorant and do not know how to take care of books, and we must teach them the value of having these books.

I know only too well how difficult it is to make the students understand this. As soon as they get the books, they sell them in the bazaar and they become lost. They leave them outside and they become dirty. They make marks in them with their pens. Therefore, it is important to make sure that the fine books printed by the ministry are not lost or ruined, for it will be a long time before we get others.

It is necessary for me to be very firm with the Keepers, and to make sure that they pay for any books they lose because of their carelessness or irresponsibility. If the Keepers in my district lose books or become subject to bribes, it is because I have not been firm enough with them.

How will I explain lazy Keepers in my district? How can I write my report and say that we gave out 1,300 books at the beginning of the year, and at the end of the year there are only 1,200? Truly, this is not good for me. The ministry has given very direct instructions to all inspectors not to tolerate lazy or irresponsible Keepers in our districts. It is necessary for our country to develop responsible people.

2

Country: Afghanistan

Issue: Who Is Expected to Pay?

Source: *Discussion Leader's Manual for Cross-Cultural Studies Training: Afghanistan.* Prepared by Rosalind Pearson and Janet Bing, Peace Corps.

This Afghan guy was in my history class and I thought it would be a good idea to speak to him once in a while as he didn't seem to have too many friends. So after class one day, I went up to him and asked him how he liked the class and a bunch of other questions, just to get going. He seemed very eager to talk—even though he didn't say much, and, as he didn't seem eager to hurry off to anything, I suggested that we go off to the Den for some coffee. He agreed right away, so we went out and got on this bus that goes around campus for a nickel, because the Den was on the other side of campus, a couple of miles away. I dropped my nickel in and headed for a seat, but the Afghan didn't follow me right away. I turned around and saw him standing at the fare box looking around uncertainly and fumbling in his pockets with about ten students behind him waiting to get on the bus. The driver was getting annoyed but the guy didn't seem to have any luck finding a nickel, so I went up and explained that he was supposed to put a nickel in the box, since it occurred to me that he might not know what to do. The driver was getting more and more impatient and I didn't think it would be so hot if he started yelling, so I put a nickel in for him figuring he could pay me back later. He seemed very relieved. When we got to the Den I ordered a sandwich with my coffee and he did the same. We talked about this and that, and when the checks came, he didn't pick his up. Well, okay, but I was glad we hadn't gone to the delicatessen where it's considerably more expensive. It also became clear that he had forgotten about the bus fare. Funny—he didn't even say "thank you" or anything when he left, although he certainly seemed to enjoy himself. After all, I did end up treating him.

3

Country:	Colombia
Issue:	Customer Service
Source:	*The Cultural Dimension of International Business.* Gary P. Ferraro. Englewood Cliffs, NJ: Prentice-Hall, 1990.

Tom Bennett, a senior accountant with a major New York accounting firm, had just arrived in Bogotá, Colombia, to assume a two-month assignment to set up an accounting procedure for a middle-sized local business. On his way to the office Tom stopped to cash a check at the main branch of the largest bank in the country where he had just opened an account a week earlier. Tom approached the least crowded teller's window, which had about eight people crowded around it. After about five minutes of jostling, Tom worked his way in front of the teller's window and handed the teller his check. But while he was waiting for his money, several other people elbowed their way up to the window and handed the teller their checks. And the teller took them. Tom was getting increasingly annoyed with the rudeness of these people who kept interrupting his banking transaction. While Tom waited for his money, a number of people kept trying to get in front of him; and what made things even more infuriating was that they seemed to be angry at him. And to think that people from the United States are always accused of being impatient. When his money finally arrived, he couldn't wait to get out of that very unfriendly situation. As he walked on to his office, he was already thinking about the letter of complaint he would send to the bank president.

How Might You Explain Tom's Frustration At The Bank?

Some Helpful Information:

This is an excellent example of what can happen if one assumes that banks in Bogotá operate under the same system as they do in Manhattan. In the United States we expect to line up in an orderly fashion and wait our turn. In most banking transactions in the United States, the teller handles the entire transaction. But in Bogotá, in the absence of a sophisticated electronic system, most checks must be verified to ensure sufficient funds to cover them. That process may take five or ten minutes under normal circumstances. Thus, it is expected in Colombia that a person will walk up to the teller directly, hand over the check, and then step aside until the check has cleared, thereby allowing others to hand their checks to the teller. When the check has cleared, the person's name will be called and he or she will be given the money. Clearly this is a very different system of customer service than would be found in the United States. Had Tom understood this very logical system, he could have avoided an unpleasant situation.

4

Country: England

Issue: American Informality

Source: *So You Speak English Too,* V. Lynn Tyler and Deborah Coon, Eds. Language and Intercultural Research Center, Brigham Young University, 1979, pp. 20-21.

You are dining with an English family, the Smythes, when you learn that a second guest is John Creighton-Forbes, an author of mystery novels, whom you greatly admire. Elated at the chance to make his acquaintance, you chat pleasantly with him and your hosts during the dinner.

After eating, you stand with Mr. Creighton-Forbes talking and taking in the view from the window. In spite of his fame, he seems like a warm and companionable man, genuinely interested in you and your life.

In your exuberance, you reach to give his shoulder a squeeze and say, "Well, John, I can't tell you how much it's meant to meet you. My wife will really be tickled when I tell her. I hope we can keep in touch."

Instantly he draws back and your hand falls to your side. You realize that you have done something wrong.

What do you do now?

1. Continue as if nothing has happened, and count on your warm personality to win him over through the rest of the evening.

2. Excuse yourself early, go home, and contact him later.

3. Forget it and cross him off. The world is full of authors.

4. When you have a private moment with him, briefly apologize for being somewhat forward; attribute it to being an American with different customs of social familiarity. Then go back to calling him "Mr. Creighton-Forbes."

Answers:

1. This is possible, but you will have trouble reachieving his esteem. You have stepped over the barrier that the English prefer to keep between themselves and new acquaintances. For them, such liberties as using first names and affectionate pats on the shoulder are earned only through long acquaintance.

2. You have given at least mild offense; it is not likely he will be too receptive in the future unless you make amends rather soon.

3. This might be necessary, especially if your pride keeps you from apologizing.

4. This is probably your best bet if you value his acquaintance or your reputation as a dinner guest.

5

Country:	Ethiopia
Issue:	Cultural Differences in Expectations
Source:	*Examples of Cross-Cultural Problems Encountered by Americans Working Overseas: An Instructor's Handbook.* E. Lord. Alexandria, VA: HumRRO, 1965.

Miss Larson

The school day ended. Tired Miss Larson took her classroom problems home with her and shared her concerns with friends at an informal cocktail party, including her frustrations over teaching in the Ethiopian government school: "For three years, I've tried to get those dear little girls to behave like normal human beings, to have some pride, to hold up their heads, look me in the face, and to answer a question in a voice I can hear without straining. They're so bright; they learn as fast as the children back home, but they're hopeless, absolutely hopeless. They just can't seem to learn to behave with human dignity. For all the good I've done here, I might as well have stayed home in Iowa and continued to teach there."

Kebedetch

The school day ended. Kebedetch walked stiffly home. The strange steel she had forced into her neck muscles seemed to have spread throughout her body. She felt rigid, brave, and frightened. Entering the *gojo* (small house or hut), Kebedetch was greeted warmly. Father asked the usual daily question. "What did you learn in school today?" Kebedetch threw back her head, looked her father in the eye, and proclaimed in a loud, clear voice, "Ethiopia is composed of twelve provinces, plus the federated state of Eritrea."

Mama and Papa talked late that night. What had happened to Kebedetch? She was no longer behaving as a normal human being. "Did you notice how she threw back her head like a man?" asked Papa. "What has happened to her shyness as a woman?" "And her voice," added Mama, "how happy I am that our parents were not present to hear a daughter of ours speak with the voice of a foreigner."

"She showed no modesty; she seemed to feel no pride. If she were normal, she would be ashamed to raise her head like that, being a girl child, and to speak so loud as that," Papa added with a deep sigh.

"Kebedetch has learned so much," said Mama, "she knows more than I, and this has given me great joy. But if her learnings are making her a strange, ungentle, beastlike person, I do not want her to learn more; she is my only daughter."

Papa pondered. Finally he shook his head and spoke. "You are right, Mebrat, our daughter must not return to school. The new education is good, but only the strongest can survive. I had hoped Kebedetch could learn and remain normal and gentle, could become a woman of dignity. This frightening behavior of hers tonight has convinced me. She has lost her sense of pride, lost her sense of shame, lost her dignity. She must never return to the school. We shall try to help her find herself again."

6

Country:	Germany
Issue:	Concept of Respect
Source:	*German-Speaking People of Europe, Building Bridges of Understanding** series, V. Lynn Tyler, Ed. Language and Intercultural Research Center, Brigham Young University, 1978, pp. 25-26.

Mr. Smith, a special guest from the United States, is about to speak to a large audience. The people seem to have enjoyed the speakers who preceded him. As he stands, Smith wants to convey his friendly feelings to the audience and put them at ease.

Assuming a somewhat casual posture with one hand in his pocket and the other grasping the podium, he tells a humorous story which he has told many times to other audiences. Other audiences have appreciated his humor, and it has served to relax them and gain their attention before he continued on in a more serious vein. This time, however, he is met with strained silence as his translator conveys his message to the group.

Shifting uneasily in front of the silent assembly, Smith continues with his speech, wondering what he has done or said wrong to create such a reaction.

What did he do?

1. His translator is most likely not giving an accurate translation of his joke.

2. He did not look at the audience directly while talking to them but gazed at the podium or ceiling.

3. He did nothing wrong. It just seemed to him as if the people were displeased. Their silence was really their way of expressing their enjoyment.

4. His casual pose and light remarks seemed disrespectful.

Answers:

1. This is possible since humor does not translate across cultures, but it is not Mr. Smith's major problem.

2. This is another possible reason. To German-speaking Europeans, undivided attention is indicated by eye contact. But, again, this is most likely not the cause of Mr. Smith's communication problem.

3. Wrong. They looked upset, and they were.

4. This is the principal reason for the cool reception Mr. Smith received. His casual attitude (especially the hand in the pocket) produced a reaction exactly opposite the one he had expected. Instead of putting the people at ease, they felt uneasy seeing Smith in a pose which to them denoted

disrespect. The disrespect seemed even greater to them because Mr. Smith was to speak about a serious topic and because he was considered an authority on the subject.

Some Helpful Information:

The German-speaking people feel that great respect should be shown in public meetings. It is disrespectful to greet even a friend on the street with your hand in your pocket.

Another problem occurred when Mr. Smith tried to be humorous. Jokes or humor are seen as being out of place in such a setting; all thoughts on the light side should be reserved for less formal occasions. Also, it must be remembered that humor doesn't always translate from culture to culture.

The Germanic concept of respect also extends to interpersonal relations. Other people's opinions are highly respected and full attention is given to a person who is speaking. Americans emphasize how likable and personable the people with whom they interact are. The better Americans know a person, the more relaxed and casual they are around that person. German speakers build their bonds on greater respect rather than greater casualness.

---

*The *Building Bridges of Understanding* series has been replaced by *Culturegrams*. *Culturegrams* are available for over 110 countries of the world. For more information, contact the David M. Kennedy Center for International Studies at Brigham Young University (1-800-528-6279).

7

Country:	India
Issue:	Work Value Differences; Volunteerism
Source:	*The Volunteer and the Bureaucrat: Case Studies from India.* Training Manual for India Volunteers. Vol. B. Prepared by Allen Bradford, Peace Corps.

When I arrived on the scene, my supervisor had absolutely no idea what I was supposed to do. I wasn't sure exactly what I was supposed to do either.

The man was very hospitable. However, he had the attitude that I should just sit around and talk and drink tea and enjoy the two years. Because of this, it's a good thing he was transferred. I'd tell him I wanted to start some project, and he'd talk me out of it.

People constantly were asking me, "How much are you making?" I'd tell them, "I'm making $55 a month, which is about 400 rupees." Then they would want to know, "How much could you make in the United States?" "Five hundred dollars," I'd say. "Well, why did you come here?" "I came here because I wanted to. I'm a volunteer." Then they would give me their "ah-ha" look.

The intensity may vary, but they all have their suspicions about us. They don't understand why I've come. They think I'm here for some ulterior motive.

8

Country: India

Issue: Understanding Another Culture's Values

Source: Unknown.

"Mother, wait a minute," Judy said to me. Something had been troubling her ever since she first came from school. "What would you say if...?" I set the plates back on the table and sat down. "What would you say if I told you I was going to become a Hindu?"

It was a good thing that I had sat down. "What did you say, Judy?" I stalled.

"What would you say if I told you I was going to become a Hindu?" She did not take her eyes off my face.

"You're not joking?" I knew she wasn't. Her deep brown eyes could not have been more serious.

"I am not joking," she said.

What was there for me to say? The sweet, earnest, devout child before me, flesh of my flesh, a Hindu! I had never thought of her in any way except as a child of Christ. I had failed her, and I had failed God. I had failed the other missionaries and our Indian Christians. How could I face anybody? All this came over me in a flash, and I was then more deeply shamed in the realization that my first reaction was one of loss of face.

She let me sit in silence until the whole impact of what she had said sank in. I saw her whole life before me including her marriage to.... Where was her father? Perhaps he would be able to cope with this.

I must have looked very stricken, for she suddenly said, "I'm sorry, Mother. I just want you to know how Rani's mother will feel. Rani is going to tell her mother, this vacation, that she is going to become a Christian. It will affect her family as deeply as it would affect you if I became a Hindu."

When I think how close *our* family has been, it makes me hurt all over to think how hers will suffer.

9

Country:	Japan
Issue:	Employer-Employee Relationships
Source:	*The Cultural Dimension of International Business.* Gary P. Ferraro. Englewood Cliffs, NJ: Prentice-Hall, 1990.

George Burgess was a chief engineer for a machinery manufacturer based in St. Louis. His company had recently signed a contract with one of its largest customers in Japan to upgrade the equipment and retrain mechanics to maintain the equipment more effectively. As part of the contract, the Japanese company sent all ten of their mechanics to St. Louis for a three-month retraining course under George's supervision. Although George had never lived or worked abroad, he was looking forward to the challenge of working with the group of Japanese mechanics, for he had been told that they were all fluent in English and tireless workers. The first several weeks of the training went along quite smoothly, but soon George became increasingly annoyed with the constant demands they were making on his personal time. They would seek him out for additional information after the regularly scheduled sessions were over. They sought his advice on how to occupy their leisure time. Several even asked him to help settle a disagreement that developed between them. Feeling frustrated by all these demands on his time, George told his Japanese trainees that he preferred not to mix business with pleasure. Within a matter of days the group requested another instructor.

Why Did The Trainees Ask For A New Instructor?

Some Helpful Information:

The employee-employer relationship in Japan is very different from that in the United States. When a Japanese firm hires an employee, he or she becomes part of the corporate family. Whereas labor and management in the United States operate largely from an adversarial perspective, the relationship between the Japanese worker and the company is based on loyalty and a long-term commitment to one another. Not only do most employees expect to stay with the firm for the duration of their careers, the firm also takes an active role in the personal lives of its employees and their families. Housing, recreation, and schooling for the children are just some of the things arranged by the employers for their workers. Moreover, there is far less separation of business and personal matters between Japanese employees and their supervisors. Thus, it is little wonder that the Japanese mechanics thought that George Burgess was not acting like a responsible supervisor because he was unwilling to become involved in their personal lives.

10

Country:	Japan
Issue:	Status
Source:	USICA In-House Case Study, U.S. International Communication Agency (presently U.S. Information Agency), Washington, DC.

A USICA research team is conducting a survey of three agency magazines in Tokyo. The contracted research company is a Gallup affiliate in Japan. The project director for this USICA-funded project is the Gallup affiliate's Japanese Director of International Operations, a very prestigious position in Japan. The director's English, while generally acceptable in written form, is very poor in conversation. The junior colleague assigned to the project, also a Japanese, has an excellent command of English, both in written and oral form. The junior colleague also seems to have a friendlier, more open manner in working with Americans.

In meetings of the entire team, composed of both Japanese and Americans, the junior colleague tends to speak very little. He seems reluctant to offer his ideas, even though they are generally quite creative. The project director speaks a great deal, but his English is barely understandable and his ideas seem tired and bureaucratic. Although his spoken English is really inadequate, he feels he does not need an interpreter. When spoken to in English, he indicates he understands, even though it is obvious to the Americans, from his inappropriate responses, that he doesn't know what has been said much of the time.

The VOA (Voice of America) radio station has become very interested in the work which the Japanese affiliate of Gallup has been carrying on in the area of Japanese public opinion of Americans. VOA program planners were impressed with the description of the affiliate's activities which they had received from the affiliate's Director of International Operations. They did not know, at the time, that the description had been written by the junior colleague, and they want to do a story on it.

You, a junior officer with USICA, have been asked to help set up an interview which will be used on an upcoming VOA breakfast show. The time scheduled for the interview is very tight, and the interviewer wants to present the best possible program. You realize it is important for the project director not to lose face and for the junior colleague not to upstage the director, but you, too, are anxious that the interview be as effective as possible.

The PAO (Public Affairs Officer, head USICA officer at post) and the American ambassador have both expressed keen interest in this project. They recognize the problems, and they are willing to help in any way they can. What plan of attack do you suggest?

11

Country:	Korea
Issue:	Collectivism
Source:	*The Cultural Dimension of International Business.* Gary P. Ferraro. Englewood Cliffs, NJ: Prentice-Hall, 1990.

Frank McDougal had been chosen to set up a branch office of his engineering consulting firm in Seoul, Korea. Although the six engineering consultants who would eventually be transferred to Seoul were all Americans, Frank was interested in hiring local support staff. He was particularly interested in hiring a local person with excellent accounting skills to handle the company's books. He was quite confident that he would be able to find the right person for the job because his company was prepared to offer an excellent salary and benefits package. After receiving what he considered to be several excellent leads from a friend at the Rotary Club, he was quite surprised to be turned down by all four prospective candidates. They were all very appreciative of being considered for the position, but they all preferred to stay with their current employers. Frank just couldn't understand why all four of these Koreans chose to pass up an increase in salary and fringe benefits.

How Would You Explain This Situation to Frank?

Some Helpful Information:

The unwillingness of these four Korean accountants to leave their current employers can be explained in terms of a basic value difference between U.S. and Korean cultures: individualism versus collectivism. Whereas workers in the United States are expected to "get ahead" by exploiting every opportunity to procure ever better jobs, the Korean philosophy is a more collective one that emphasizes dedication and loyalty to the group (that is, firm) rather than individual achievement. Individuals gain their own sense of importance primarily through the prestige of the group to which they belong. Moreover, a large segment of a Korean employee's life revolves around the workplace. The Korean employee gives great loyalty to the collective (that is, employer) and in return expects support and loyalty from the employer. It is for this reason that most Koreans stay with their initial employer for their entire careers and seldom change jobs even with the lure of higher pay and increased benefits.

12

Country:	Korea
Issue:	Role Inequality
Source:	From a compilation of Peace Corps Volunteer Case Studies on Korea.

Part I

When I first came to Korea I had no real grasp of the place of women in the society. In training I had heard a great deal about it. But perhaps you have to experience something like that before you really understand it. My expectations were far removed from the reality of the situation.

When we first arrived as volunteers in our province to teach English, we had difficulty maintaining our volunteer standing. Gifts and money were being pushed at us from everyone who wanted our help. Our first refusal and explanation usually convinced most of them. However, our provincial board of education was tireless in finding ways to give us money. In the guise of travel reimbursements it would try to pay us thousands of *won*. We explained, pleaded, and finally refused completely to accept anything.

It was at this point in our relationship with the board that I had my most serious run-in with Mr. Lee, my coteacher.

My deficiency in the Korean language often made me dependent on Mr. Lee. I was very uncomfortable because he seemed to be exploiting the situation. He opened my account at the bank and helped me prepare background information about myself for the school. He used these opportunities to find out what kind of job I'd had at home and what my salary had been. I later discovered that this was not part of the necessary background information which the school had requested.

When people came to see me at school, I had no interpreter but Mr. Lee. He carried on interviews as if I weren't present. Some of them appeared in the newspaper and, when translated, were found to contain inaccurate information.

I became very wary and guarded around Mr. Lee. I knew that anything that hurt me would hurt Mr. Lee much more, since he was the sole teacher responsible for me. Also, I knew my best interests and his were the same. But I was still suspicious.

On this particular morning, Mr. Lee rushed to my desk and said the office needed my seal (a special stamp that substitutes for one's signature). I asked why they needed it. He replied that he didn't know exactly but there were papers that had to have my seal. I should have gone myself, but I was busy so I handed it to him. He returned moments later with 2,400 won and an explanation. The money was a padded payment from the board, for which I had signed by the use of my seal. Mr.

Lee, well aware of our quarrel with the board, laughed at my anger and the little joke he had played on me.

After this incident I had as little to do with Mr. Lee as possible. I scrupulously kept him out of my affairs. He was offended and probably a little confused by this.

Part II

At about the time the new semester began, Mr. Lee was transferred to another school. After he left, I learned that he had done much to help me during my first month there. Much of the enthusiasm for my English conversation class was enthusiasm he had generated for me. The motivation of the advanced classes was motivation he had stimulated.

Looking back I can understand his actions a little better. He could not offer me friendship because friendship only exists between equals. We weren't equals—I was a woman—and a young unmarried one at that. So he could not approach me directly in any situation. He needed to use deceptive means in dealing with me to retain his conception of what the relationship should be. He needed to keep abreast and ahead of the "news" about me—so he found out what he could through deception. He couldn't converse with me as an equal. He needed to make it clear that it was he who ran me and not I who ran him, so he couldn't interpret for me. It was easier to trick me into actions like accepting the money than trying to persuade me to take it as he would have had to do in his role as coteacher.

There are many things Mr. Lee and I could have shared had we been friends. We could have learned much from each other. The status of women got in the way.

13

Country: Korea

Issue: Cultural Differences in Social Roles

Source: From a compilation of Peace Corps Volunteer Case Studies on Korea.

Soon after we arrived at our teaching assignments in Korea, my husband went on the fall picnic. The students scattered along the mountainside to sing and joke, and the teachers retired to a small house to drink. At this point, my husband was introduced to the Korean custom of exchanging wine cups. As a newcomer, he was the prime target for exchanges, and not knowing how to refuse without offending—and also eager to show his drinking capabilities—he drank more than his share.

Not much later, the same thing happened after an athletic contest at his school. People at the school began calling him a "famous drunkard," though they enjoyed drinking with him. He soon realized this wasn't quite the image he wanted to project (and didn't like Korean wine that much anyway), so he curbed his drinking activities.

During this time my husband's coteachers in his department were regularly inviting him to go out to dinner at one restaurant or another, and I accompanied them. I was always the only woman present, and though we repeatedly asked them to bring their wives along, I remained the only woman. After a number of such occasions, we became the object of their jokes. My husband was henpecked because I had made him stop drinking and wouldn't let him go out during the week drinking with the men. I was also the domineering American wife who controlled her husband and refused to stay at home. We became quite uncomfortable, and when the teachers had apparently had their fun, their invitations suddenly ceased.

Now, our only Korean social companions are our language tutors—a Korean couple our age, well educated. He had been to the United States. They are extremely unusual as they enjoy going to dinner, the movies, and parties as a couple.

14

Country:	Korea
Issue:	Maintaining Harmony; Saving Face
Source:	*The Cultural Dimension of International Business.* Gary P. Ferraro. Englewood Cliffs, NJ: Prentice-Hall, 1990.

Jim Ellis, vice president of a North Carolina knitwear manufacturer, was sent by his company to observe firsthand how operations were proceeding in its Korean plant and to help institute some new managerial procedures. Before any changes could be made, however, Jim wanted to learn as much as possible about the problems that existed at the plant. During his first weeks he was met with bows, polite smiles, and the continual denial of any significant problems. But Jim was enough of a realist to know that no manufacturing operation is without its problems. So after some creative research, he uncovered a number of problems that the local manager and staff were not acknowledging. None of the problems was particularly unusual or difficult to solve. But Jim was frustrated that no one would admit that any problems existed. "If you don't acknowledge the problems," he complained to one of the managers, "how do you expect to be able to solve them?" To further exasperate him, when a problem *was* finally brought to his attention, it was not mentioned until the end of the work day, when there was no time left to solve it.

How Could You Help Jim Better Understand the Dynamics of the Situation?

Some Helpful Information:

Asians in general, and Koreans in particular, place a high value on harmonious personal relationships. Conflicts are avoided at all costs and every effort is made to be polite and nonconfrontational. Also, Koreans have great difficulty in admitting failure, for to do so is to be humiliated or shamed, that is, to lose face. It is therefore important to maintain a high degree of *kibun*, translated as "morale" or "self-esteem." The reporting or acknowledging of a problem is far more serious than the problem itself, for it causes a loss of face for the teller and a loss of morale for the hearer. Thus, when the Korean employees withheld knowledge about plant problems from Jim, they did so to (1) preserve his kibun and (2) not lose face themselves. If anything negative has to be reported it should be done, according to the Korean way, at the end of the day so the parties involved will at least have the evening to restore their damaged kibun.

15

Area: Middle East (General)

Issue: Conflict between Islamic and Western Values in the Classroom

Source: Unknown. (This is an authentic letter from an American who had spent approximately two years in an Arab country.)

Dear Ed:

Sometimes I'm convinced that I've been teaching English in this little Moslem town too long for my own good.

The whole social structure of this country tends to undermine the goals of the Western scholar. Logical thought processes, on which most Western teachers rely instinctively, have just never been taught here. Deductive reasoning is unheard of. The teacher is thought of only as a lecturer and a recorder; what he teaches is not original—it has been true from the beginning of time and known since the time of Mohammed. The teacher has made no discoveries of his own and will make none; but, as he has been fortunate enough to have been taught, he is in turn privileged to reteach what he has learned. As truth is unchanging, there is nothing to discuss or question. The teaching process is a continuation of the oral tradition; what has been learned in the past is now transmitted verbatim to the student who writes it down and memorizes it. This method, however, is more than tradition: it is dictated by the nature of the cosmos and can only be the repetition of what Allah revealed to Mohammed, the last and greatest of Allah's prophets. There is no other way of knowing. As original knowledge does not exist, the most reliable way to learn is through the same medium and by the same technique by which knowledge has been acquired in the past.

Accordingly, there is no discussion and no personal opinion in the Moslem classroom. The teacher either reads to the students from his notes or from a book, and they copy in their notebooks what is read to them. Sometimes a student is substituted for the teacher and he reads to the boys. No papers of any kind are ever written, and there is no questioning the teacher. To these people there is only one truth; the idea that two "experts" might interpret the same facts in opposite ways is inconceivable to them. An American teacher once "proved" to his class that 1 equalled 2. No one objected, and the students all wrote the proof down in their notebooks. The teacher had shown it to them; therefore, it must be true. There is no distrusting the conveyor of the source of truth.

In this society it is the form, not the content, that is important, and herein lies the most significant problem that the Western teacher has to deal with. In the Moslem scale of values it is not so important that a student cannot know seventeen subjects at once, as long as the curriculum makes it look like he is learning them. It is not so important that the students have a high rate of absenteeism as long as the books show full attendance [the same is true of teacher attendance]. Thus, the passing grade of 35%, though in reality showing an inferior knowledge of the subject, is in practice considered adequate. A boy with 70% knowledge is considered very good. The student himself does not feel that learning itself is important; what is important to him is the card that shows the teacher has given him a passing grade. The common concept is that the teacher gives you a grade; you do not earn it. This is not to say, of course, that the same phenomena do not exist elsewhere; it is to say only that they predominate in this country. A boy with a 35% to 50% grade in the United States, for example, does not kid himself that he has learned very much, and indeed may consider, with regret, that he missed a good opportunity to learn. Here the question of learning or not learning rarely comes to mind.

A concomitant problem is the one of cheating in the classroom. There is rarely a test of any kind given during which cheating does not occur, for in the Moslem classroom it is almost literally true that it is sufficient for only one student to understand the lesson. One of the five pillars of Islam is almsgiving, the aid one gives to those whom Allah has made less fortunate. The concept of almsgiving pervades all aspects of life. Thus cheating, and by extension bribing, nepotism, etc., are not looked at as being morally wrong in the way that they are in the Western world. To the Moslem, it is an obvious fact that Allah has made some people more intelligent than others, and, in a sense, classroom performance is preordained; there is no feeling that hard work may enable one to pass by his own efforts, make him a better person, etc.; there is only the feeling that, unaided, many will fail and that it is thus a duty to pass on knowledge to the less fortunate ones. In fact, the teachers themselves aid and abet the cheating by lax observation during exams, for a good class record reflects favorably on their abilities as teachers!

Unfortunately, cheating occurs not only on exams, but also on a day-to-day classroom basis. On this level, it is a mechanism to "save face." When the teacher calls on a student, he is expected to know something. In most cases it is recitation of some kind that is required. Usually the student listens to a student behind him who, with open book, is reading him the answer. By this means of prompting, a student may go a whole year without the teacher ever realizing that in reality he knows nothing. Homework is usually ineffective because the students refuse to struggle with it. Instead, another student or a brother or relative will do it. Behind these external manifestations we again find different values. Actual gains are subordinated to surface appearances.

Intrinsically related to this network of social and religious values is their attitude toward individual effort. It must be pointed out here that their attitude is a realistic one in terms of their culture, yet one which the Western teacher reacts against and must cope with. Life is tough in the Middle East; a lot of work often means little or no change. Thus, sometime in the past, in order to better live with themselves and the harsh world around them, these people came to feel that individual effort, in most cases, comes to naught. In reality, in this part of the world, effort does not count; it is Allah who determines what is or is not to be achieved.

Essentially this means that the end rather than the means is of value, while to the westerner, more often than not, it is the other way around. Again, it is the problem of the form being more important than the content. As mentioned previously, there is no feeling in the classroom that hard work and proper questions—in short, an all-out effort to understand instead of memorize—might bring about some kind of good, either in grades or in other less tangible ways. Many of the students are capable of and willing to do hard work, but feel it worthwhile only in the drudging path of learning by rote, which they are used to. It is the hard work of thinking that they balk at, the work of understanding that A plus B does not equal A plus B, but equals C, a third object that has to be deduced, not memorized.

What must be emphasized is that many of these above-mentioned values make sense in terms of the society and are wrong only as far as they conflict with Western values as possessed by the Western teacher. For a Western teacher to feel he is accomplishing something he must to some extent instill his own values in his students, for they are the only things he can measure by. What is hard for him to face is the degree to which these American values do not and cannot pervade Moslem life and the realization of the chances against his success. When he realizes that his students are never face-to-face with any other than their country's values, except, perhaps, in that forty minutes a day he is teaching English, he is bound to feel he is fighting a losing battle. He sees that he cannot afford to teach only English, he must go beyond this to create attitudes and values which are exactly opposite his students' own. The student sees from his father that hard work and individual effort count for little, while he sees from his uncle that cheating and bribing lead to the top. He knows that being a relative of nobility is far more important than being intelligent, and he knows that the boy next to him will pass because his father is an important man. Therefore, he might as well show his paper to him and retain a friend. In the long run, it is he, and not the Western teacher, who knows how things are done and who will succeed and who will not succeed.

The greatest problem comes when the Western teacher begins to see the logic of Islamic values. He begins to doubt himself and becomes too sympathetic to the plight of his students. He is in danger of being half-Easternized himself.

All the best,

Bob

16

Area:	North Africa
Issue:	Problem of Being a Single Woman in North Africa
Source:	*Letters from North Africa,* Gordon Schimmel, Ed. Volunteer Liaison Officer, Division of Volunteer Support, Division of University Relations and Training and the Office of Programming and Planning. Peace Corps, 1966.

Dear Jen:

My roommate and I teach at a boarding school. The students are well disciplined, and there has never been any question as to my authority, either in class or after hours. I'm paid all the respect I could possibly want. I have a satisfactory image, and I suspect that my presence there has done more good than harm.

As a part of the community, however, the value of my presence is highly questionable. Typical host-country nationals who learn that I live alone with another girl, am single, and teach at a boys' school, suffer absolute misunderstanding. They ask, "What bad thing did she do, that she was sent here? Obviously from a very bad family. What kind of parents would allow this? And she went to school, too! She has a number of visitors, all of them men, and she blatantly looks you in the face as she buys your onions. Such disgraceful dress. Thank God we keep our women in their place—at home."

I can't fight being thought of as a prostitute. How does one prove she's not a witch? Nearly everything I do to disprove them has the opposite effect. Suppose I meet an employee at the airline office and he invites me to his house to meet his family, and I accept, hoping to meet an entire household of people and, perhaps, establish the beginnings of a rewarding friendship. But the employee in the office knows what he is doing—he knows the conditions of his invitation much better than I, and I've only reinforced what he thought all along. Oblivious, I drag my roommate along to meet what we both are sure will be a typical host-country family, as was promised. We find ourselves in a room with two men. When we ask to see the women, they come in briefly, talk little, and soon leave. The evening drags on. When we leave, our hands are squeezed, even kissed, and we're invited back for the next night. As we back out, the bulbs in our heads suddenly brighten, and we are appalled to realize that we've inadvertently led them on.

Women are sealed off from us. We have precious few chances to meet them, and then it's usually through a husband, which gets us off on the wrong foot immediately. I can just about count on being considered a potential mistress by both the man and his wife. Whether I'm an undesirable companion, whether wives don't want me making a fool of myself and their husbands, or whether they would like to know me, I don't know. I rather suspect that they care very little about seeing me after an initial curiosity because my pattern of living is far outside their range of experience or possibility. I fetch about the same interest as a baby gorilla—fascinating, but a monster, nevertheless.

Growl!

Julie

17

Area:	North Africa
Issue:	Expectations of Americans
Source:	*Letters from North Africa*, Gordon Schimmel, Ed. Volunteer Liaison Officer, Division of Volunteer Support, Division of University Relations and Training and the Office of Programming and Planning. Peace Corps, 1966.

An official of the Ministry of Education visited my secondary school and noticed that the PCVs located at the school were riding bicycles to school while the host-country teachers and expatriates were riding *Mobylettes* and scooters, and some were even arriving in cars.

Later he commented to me that he thought it would be more appropriate for us to make use of similar transportation, rather than to appear each morning riding on bikes like schoolboys.

I explained that it is Peace Corps policy that we not own a motorized vehicle, and we are encouraged to use bicycles since we live a good distance from the school.

He replied that this was unrealistic and foolish. "Everyone," he says, "expects Americans to own *cars*! Didn't the Americans invent the car?"

I answered him by saying, "If PCVs owned scooters or cars, it would remove them from the level of the ordinary North Africans, and we would begin to seem like 'Ugly Americans.'"

"You are not like ordinary North Africans," he stated, "you are professional people hired by the government to do a job. And the government expects efficiency from you, not acrobatics on bikes."

18

Country: The Philippines

Issue: Hospitality

Source: *The Peace Corps Volunteer in the Philippines.* Prepared by Lone Castillo and Paul Boriack, Volumes A and B. Peace Corps.

The Paterno family has accepted you as their new daughter. They express a great deal of concern over your being well taken care of.

When you arrived, the family had a big party. The meals since have been lavish. The food is so delicious and the meals so large and frequently offered that you are rapidly gaining weight.

On several occasions you have raised the question of payment for board with Mrs. Paterno. Her reaction has varied from being slightly insulted, although good-humored, to vague remarks about settling the matter by and by, or that you can pay whatever you like.

Your teachers have indicated that P50 per month is a fair price. You offer this to Mrs. Paterno and she flatly refuses.

19

Country:	The Philippines
Issue:	Invasion of Privacy
Source:	*People of the Philippines, Building Bridges of Understanding* series, V. Lynn Tyler, Ed. Language and Intercultural Research Center, Brigham Young University, 1977, p. 15.

"Are you all moved into your new apartment now?" Teresita asked.

"Yes. I think I'll like it a lot," Sylvia replied.

"What do you do when you finish work?" Teresita continued.

"Oh, lots of things." Sylvia was becoming annoyed.

"And does your family approve of your living alone?"

"They don't mind." Sylvia searched for a way to end the conversation quickly. "Excuse me, I must help this customer," she said, and hurried to the front of the bank.

Sylvia had been at work only two days since transferring from the U.S. to the Philippine branch of the bank she worked for. She was doing the same job she'd done in America, though there were some variations in procedure. She was glad to learn the new techniques and have errors pointed out by Teresita, her superior. But every conversation they had about some problem seemed to go on and on and ultimately got very personal, with Teresita asking questions and discussing subjects that had nothing to do with their work at the bank.

"I hardly know her, and here she is prying into everything I do," Sylvia thought angrily. "I'll just have to tell her next time that it's none of her business."

Some Helpful Information:

Actually, by asking personal questions Teresita meant to show her concern for Sylvia.

Filipinos highly value *pakikisama*—the art of smooth interpersonal relationships. Ideally one accomplishes his or her purposes without conflict, direct confrontation, or injury to another's *amor propio*.

Amor propio refers to the Filipino's extreme sensitivity, individual esteem or dignity, and fragile sense of worth. Each Filipino sees another as a very sensitive individual who can be easily offended.

One way Filipinos attempt to minimize hurt and unpleasantness is by inquiring into another person's private life. After giving some form of criticism, the Filipino boss may follow with questions about an employee's family and personal affairs. This relieves the employee and makes her feel she still belongs and is accepted. Sometimes a personal question is asked merely as a matter of courtesy—a hotel clerk, for example, may ask a guest "Where are you going?" every time he leaves the hotel. Such an inquiry is simply a greeting—couched in more personal terms than Americans are used to—and carries no more significance than the American question, "How are you?"

20

Country: Portugal

Issue: Concept of Time

Source: *The Cultural Dimension of International Business*. Gary P. Ferraro.
             Englewood Cliffs, NJ: Prentice-Hall, 1990.

Fred Gardener, a 31-year-old sales manager for a small boat-building firm in Connecticut, decided to stop off in Lisbon to call on several potential clients after a skiing trip to Switzerland. Having set up three appointments in two days, he arrived for the first two scheduled meetings at the appointed times but was kept waiting for over a half hour in each instance. Based on these two experiences, Fred assumed that the Portuguese, like other "Latin" types, must be *mañana* oriented and not particularly concerned with the precise reckoning of time. With this in mind, he was not particularly concerned about being on time for his third appointment. Instead, he extended his visit to the local museum and arrived at his third appointment more than forty minutes late. However, Fred sensed that the Portuguese businessperson was quite displeased with his tardiness.

How Would You Explain This Reaction?

Some Helpful Information:

The meaning of time and punctuality varies not only from culture to culture but also within any culture, depending on the *social context*. In Portugal a person of high status should never be kept waiting by a person of lesser status. A woman may keep a man waiting, but it would be considered very bad form for a man to keep a woman waiting; an older person can be late for an appointment with a younger person, but the reverse is not true. Although punctuality for its own sake is not valued in the same absolute sense as it is in the United States, there are some social situations that demand punctuality and others that do not.

21

Country:	Saudi Arabia
Issue:	Business Etiquette
Source:	*The Cultural Dimension of International Business.* Gary P. Ferraro. Englewood Cliffs, NJ: Prentice-Hall, 1990.

Bill Nugent, an international real estate developer from Dallas, had made a 2:30 P.M. appointment with Mr. Abdullah, a high-ranking government official in Riyadh, Saudi Arabia. From the beginning things did not go well for Bill. First, he was kept waiting until nearly 3:45 before he was ushered into Mr. Abdullah's office. When he finally did get in, several other men were also in the room. Even though Bill felt that he wanted to get down to business with Mr. Abdullah, he was reluctant to get too specific because he considered much of what they needed to discuss sensitive and private. To add to Bill's sense of frustration, Mr. Abdullah seemed more interested in engaging in meaningless small talk than in dealing with substantive issues concerning their business.

How Might You Help Bill Deal With His Frustration?

Some Helpful Information:

Saudis do not budget their time in the same way that Americans do. Time is considered to be a much more flexible commodity. The best piece of advice we might give Bill is to be patient and allow more time when conducting business affairs in Saudi Arabia than would be normal in the United States. Moreover, what Bill considered to be "small talk" is a very important part of the process of doing business in Saudi Arabia. Trust is an important ingredient in business affairs. Before engaging in meaningful business relations, most Saudis need time to get to know those with whom they are about to do business. They feel that there is no better way to do this than to discuss a wide variety of nonbusiness topics while drinking coffee. Finally, Saudis define private and public space somewhat differently than they do in Dallas, Texas. Although Saudis are extremely private in their personal lives, they are quite open in those things they consider to be public, and business is thought to fall into the public domain. Thus, even though the Western businessperson may want to discuss confidential business matters, it is not at all uncommon for a "personal" appointment to be conducted with other people in the room.

22

Country: Spain

Issue: Influence of Religion

Source: *España, Building Bridges of Understanding* series, V. Lynn Tyler, Ed. Language and Intercultural Research Center, Brigham Young University, 1977, p. 18.

You are to supervise a project that must be completed by a specific deadline. Every available working day must be used in order to finish on time. You've been asked to plan a work schedule that will guarantee the completion of the project by the specified date. You have planned for the workers to have Sundays free.

Reviewing your projected work schedule, a Spanish work supervisor points out that the duration of the project will include three Catholic holidays. All three occur in the middle of the workweek and are marked by festive celebrations.

What can you do?

1. Hire only people who agree to forgo the holidays and work every day, Monday through Saturday, to complete the project.

2. Check with your supervisors on the possibility of receiving a three-day extension of the completion date for the project so that all workers can enjoy the holidays.

3. Give employees the option of working overtime on weekdays or three Saturdays to make up hours lost by attending the festivities.

Answers:

1. Most Spaniards are Catholics. You may find some willing to agree to your conditions, but there are definitely some more reasonable alternatives.

2. This is the best first alternative to try. If your superiors are aware of the cultural importance of the Spanish religious celebrations, they should be willing to adjust the completion date if possible. If they are unable to grant an extension, what should be the next step?

3. If they have been previously informed of the tight deadline, many workers will be willing to work overtime to make up for days missed. Be sure to acquaint yourself with the customs of the locality. Some smaller communities are very traditional, and it would be a serious breach of tradition for someone to work instead of participating in the religious commemoration. In some larger, more industrialized centers people may not be adverse to working during the holiday.

23

Country:	Thailand
Issue:	The Hierarchical Family
Source:	*People of Thailand, Building Bridges of Understanding* series, V. Lynn Tyler, Ed. Language and Intercultural Research Center, Brigham Young University, 1978, p. 10.

Helen was the daughter of an American businessman who supervised the establishment of a new business in Thailand. Her family lived in Thailand for a year. Some of the first friends she made were Naiyana and her sister Niramon.

When she first visited their home, Helen was introduced to Mr. and Mrs. Chaimongkol and to a younger brother, Damrong. Also living with the family was Mr. Chaimongkol's father. When Helen's family lived in the United States, her grandparents did not live nearby. Occasionally they visited Helen's family. The older woman was loved and respected, but was generally treated as a guest in the home.

One of the first adjustments Helen had to make to Thai culture was the custom of grandparents living with families, which, it seemed to her, only compounded their crowded living conditions. She was even more surprised to learn that the grandfather was actually considered the family head, and that his opinion was always sought when important decisions were to be made.

Helen remembered how on one occasion she was visiting with Naiyana when the father came home from work. He was enthusiastic about a new opportunity for a business investment which he had just learned about. He sought out his father and related the details of the venture to him. After some deliberation, the grandfather stated that he did not think the investment wise. To Helen's amazement Mr. Chaimongkol accepted his father's opinion and said he wouldn't go forward with his plans.

"Maybe my dad would talk to Grandpa about an idea," Helen remarked to herself at the time, "but he sure wouldn't let Grandpa push him around. He'd make his own decision."

Some Helpful Information:

The family unit in Thailand is a miniature political unit within Thai society. The system is hierarchical in nature, with the eldest male in charge of the unit. When he dies, the oldest female heads the unit.

The leader of the family, whether it be the grandfather, father, grandmother, or eldest son, is expected to conduct his or her life in a proper manner at all times and to be an example of a true follower of Buddhist principles. The system is not a democratic one. All family members are expected to abide by decisions of the ruling elder. The members of the family obey the family leader and many of their life's activities and decisions are determined by him or her. The loyalty and obedience of family members facilitate the smooth operation of the family unit. Since children are taught to respect their elders, it is still very common for adults to ask permission or advice from their parents.

24

Country:	Tunisia
Issue:	The American Drive to Work and Produce
Source:	*Letters from North Africa*, Gordon Schimmel, Ed. Volunteer Liaison Officer, Division of Volunteer Support, Division of University Relations and Training and the Office of Programming and Planning. Peace Corps, 1966.

While sitting in a cafe with a few Tunisian coteachers, Tom mentions that he is interested in buying pottery which is produced in a nearby village and sold in the local *medina* (bazaar). He explains that he has little idea where the pottery is sold, and one of the coteachers offers to take him there.

The next day during lunch Tom and the Tunisian teacher set off for the medina, and upon finding the pottery, the Tunisian proceeds to bargain for Tom, "so that Tom will get a *bon prix*,"—one lower than that which most tourists have to pay. The transaction completed, they go to a nearby cafe, drink some tea, and talk over teaching experiences at school. The Tunisian then suggests that they meet at the cinema the next afternoon after classes and invites Tom to a party which is to be held at a friend's house following the film. Tom accepts, a bit reluctantly, knowing that he still has papers to correct and an exam to write for the end of the week.

Following the cinema the next evening, Tom and his Tunisian friend arrive to find the party well under way. A few people are playing cards or just sitting and talking, while most of the group is twisting to French versions of American rock 'n' roll records. The group is all male. After refusing several invitations to twist, Tom decides to be a sport and dance.

Upon making his effort for "the Corps" and talking for a while, Tom explains that it is already late and he still has papers to correct and an exam to write. Despite protests from his friend and the others, Tom leaves, assuring everyone that he enjoyed the party and would love to stay, but simply has too much work to do.

The next day at lunch Tom's friend informs him that he is hurt because Tom left the party so early and that he insulted the host by not staying until the food was served. The Tunisian teacher explains, however, that fortunately he was able to explain Tom's departure and in spite of it all the group would like Tom to go to the beach with them on Sunday—the day Tom planned to correct the exam.

25

Country: Turkey

Issue: Classroom Discipline

Source: *A Case Study of Teaching in Turkey: Some Problems Faced by Peace Corps Volunteers.* Prepared by the American Institutes for Research, 1966.

I had arrived on a Saturday and classes began the following Monday; I really felt pushed. Although the textbook for each class contained all of the material to be presented during the year, it was left to the teachers to develop their own schedules and lesson plans. Because I wasn't really sure of either myself or my classes, planning was a hard chore and took up most of my free time. The Turks, meanwhile, were sparing no effort to make me feel at home. Often I wished there were fewer invitations so that I could get organized and try to find out what I was doing.

As I grew more familiar with the children in my classes, my struggles with lesson plans increased. Each class had kids with such varying levels of competence that I couldn't find a level that suited them all. It was hard to tell what level they were at; the kids seemed shy and hesitated to volunteer answers to my questions. Although I knew the Turkish teachers were very formal in the classroom, I smiled a lot and tried to show friendly encouragement to get some response from my quiet students. I got the feeling many of them were just sitting through the classes and never did their homework. Puzzled, I asked Ekrem Bey (Bey is equivalent to Mr.), the lycée math teacher, how I could get some response. "When they grow accustomed to you, they will respond," he assured me. "Most of them have never seen an American before. You are strange to them."

Determined to reach the kids and capture their interest, I slaved over my lesson preparations, trying to make English interesting. Without realizing it, I was trying to run an American class in a Turkish school.

Ekrem Bey was right. I got response—too much of it. The first to blow up was the second-year class at the trade school. I'd been trying to get them to understand the purpose of oral drills. I hadn't been able to put it across with my limited Turkish, so I had prepared visual displays showing the difficult points in each lesson. Then we'd do drills on those points. One day toward the end of the fourth week of school, as I turned away from the class to hang up the drill charts, the response came. Without any warning, everyone started talking at once.

Rapping my pencil on the desk I said, "Please, let's have quiet." The sound diminished but did not stop. There were seventy-five students, sitting three to a desk, and I couldn't spot who was continuing the disturbance. Raising my voice over the persistent rumble, I started a drill. "The pencil is on the desk. Everyone please repeat."

A few of the kids in the front rows started to recite "The pencil is…" when a falsetto voice called out from the back of the room, "Zee peenceel ees annzee…," deliberately distorting the vocal sounds. Like the cheering section at a football game, the kids in the back rows picked it up and chanted, "Zee peenceel ees…," while others laughed, talked, and shoved one another's books on the floor.

I wasn't sure I knew who the original culprit was, but I couldn't let them get away with that. I called Ali Adivar, who seemed to be the leader of the cheering section, to come to the blackboard and write the drill as the rest of the class recited. Protesting, "*Hocam* (esteemed one), I did not do it. It was Kemal, not me," he walked slowly to the board. By the time the class ended, I had twelve kids lined up writing furiously and no room for any more, but the horseplay kept up.

One by one, each of my classes "responded." I had a battle on my hands nearly every hour. Pop quizzes, difficult questions designed to humiliate the troublemakers, lectures, threats—nothing worked. I wasn't teaching them much English, and it was clear that I didn't have their respect.

Finally, I sent some offenders to the *Mudar* (principal) *Bey's* office. This had a calming effect for a little while, but I couldn't quite take the hand-kissing apologies that Mudar Bey insisted they give me. Discussing the problem with the Turkish teachers wasn't too helpful either. As Ekrem Bey put it, "The flesh belongs to the teacher; the bones to the father." In short, slug the worst offenders. I found this more distasteful than having my hand kissed.

I tried to explain to Ekrem Bey: "Hitting a student is very difficult for me. I am not criticizing your way, but I am not used to such a different method of disciplining children, and I can't bring myself to do it."

He seemed to understand and replied, "If it is difficult for you, perhaps you might enlist one of the larger boys to act as your proctor. It is not uncommon for Turkish teachers to curb the troublemakers in that way. Of course, the student would expect that his work would be viewed more kindly…. " This sounded as if I would be depending on a bully and one who had to be bribed at that! The idea wasn't at all appealing and I didn't try it.

One day after the second-year students at the trade school had been unusually noisy, even for them, Mudar Bey came in to the room. He studied my wall charts, and we talked about them for a bit. Then he asked, "Are your students being more cooperative? You haven't sent any to my office lately." What could I say, "I feel silly when they kiss my hand"? I mumbled something about trying to work it out, but I don't think he doubted for a minute the real reason for my change in strategy. Fortunately, it was time for me to go over to the lycée for my afternoon classes, so I thanked him for his concern and escaped.

As I walked along I puzzled over what I could do. If the uproars so common in my classroom were disrupting work in other rooms, I might not get the chance to handle the problem myself. If I didn't stop the chaos, I'd never teach anything.

Was Mudar Bey just trying to encourage me or was he warning me? Somehow I had to do something.

The weeks dragged by. On Mondays and Thursdays I hated to get up. That was when I taught—using the word in its loosest possible sense—the trade school second-year class. Thursdays were especially bad; I had them for a double session. Then came the week of rain. Appropriately, it started on a Thursday and poured down all day without letup. My apartment was cold and damp, and there was mildew in the closet. All my shoes were wet, and even though I stuffed them with newspaper and singed them on the wood stove, the insides did not dry out. My bed felt like a slab in the morgue.

At ten o'clock on the eighth day of rain, I collided with the second-year class. For fifteen minutes I had been trying to get their attention. No longer was I smiling at them and encouraging them; I just wanted them to keep quiet. Kemal, who really wasn't such a bad kid, had finally gotten the hang of a new sound and had been chanting, to himself, "Blue, blue, blue," over and over. I'd just convinced him to stop and practice later when Ali Adivar, who sat directly in front of my desk where I could keep an eye on him, began, "Blue-ue-ue-ue, Blue-ue-ue..." It was funny; nonetheless, when the class roared with laughter, something snapped. I pulled Ali out of his chair and shook him. He sidled back to his seat. Turning to face the class, I found, to my amazement, a look of respect in their eyes. It seemed to say, "Well, you've finally wised up!"

I didn't feel wised up. I felt depressed, and I couldn't stop my knees and voice from shaking. But the remainder of the class hour did go surprisingly well.

26

Country: U.S.A.

Issue: Self-reliance

Source: Kay T. C. Clifford, University of Michigan.

Yugo Nobuta, a Japanese student in the U.S., had an appointment with his academic adviser to discuss his graduate program. Half an hour before the appointment, a friend called and needed a ride to the airport. Yugo took his friend to the airport and was forty-five minutes late to the appointment. Luckily, his adviser, Mr. Bender, was still in his office. Yugo knocked on the door, announced himself, and went in. Mr. Bender offered him a seat, but was not friendly or talkative. Yugo had not had an academic adviser before and did not know what to expect, so he waited for the adviser to advise him. After some minutes of talking about the weather and Ann Arbor, Mr. Bender asked Yugo what he wanted to do with his program. This was a silly question to Yugo because he wanted to get his degree, of course. Then Mr. Bender asked Yugo if he had read the department's program handout which listed all the graduate requirements. Yugo was not sure which paper this was, so he said, "Yes." Mr. Bender waited, and Yugo waited. After a few minutes, the adviser asked if Yugo had made out his election worksheet. The next step, Mr. Bender explained, was for him to sign the sheet so Yugo could get registered. Yugo said, "Yes," again although he had no idea which paper this was either. Mr. Bender was holding out his hand though and obviously expected Yugo to put something into it. Yugo did not know whether to give him something or shake hands, so he handed the adviser the armful of papers he had been given by various people since arriving at the university. At this point Mr. Bender was making loud exhaling noises. He handed the papers back to Yugo. Then he rummaged around on his desk and found a small slip of paper which he told Yugo was the election worksheet. Yugo was to pick out the courses he wanted to take, fill in the slip of paper, and come back for the adviser's signature. Mr. Bender then handed Yugo a stapled document which he said was the department's degree requirements. He said that Yugo should read this before filling out the election worksheet and before making another appointment with him. The adviser stood up and Yugo correctly interpreted this as an indication that the appointment was at an end. He stood up, shook hands with Mr. Bender, and left the office. Both felt the appointment had been unsatisfactory. Yugo later told his friends that his adviser had not been very friendly or helpful and that he would see him as little as possible. The adviser told his department chair that he really didn't want to have very many more foreign students because they took too much time.

What Assumptions And Behaviors Helped Create This Miscommunication?

Resource 17

Evaluation

To evaluate the effectiveness of the materials presented in this workshop module, a number of approaches are suggested, the first one being more traditional than the others. Whichever method you choose, you may want to bring out and compare the evaluation with the expectation sheets developed at the beginning of the workshop. (See Resource 2.)

Participant Rating Form/Feedback Form

Simple participant rating forms, administered at the end of the workshop, are familiar to most facilitators. It must be pointed out, however, that this approach provides little more than a rough measure of the "satisfaction level" of those who took part. Yet for your purposes, that may suffice.

The form which follows should require no more than fifteen to twenty minutes for each participant to complete. Except for the last couple of items (which are open-ended), a check placed in the appropriate box is all that is required; the results can be tallied easily and a considerable amount of useful information provided in very short order. It is also a simple matter to compare one particular iteration of the course with any other.

After the form is administered, the items on page one should be tallied on a master sheet on which all the individual participants' scores are placed. Then circle the category with the majority of votes to obtain a general consensus reading for each exercise.

The following form, originally developed and validated by Alan Kotok, has been adapted with suggestions from Sandra Mumford Fowler.

Participant Feedback Form

Please answer the following questions so we can learn your reactions to this program to help us improve future programs. Most questions require only a check [✓] in the appropriate space. You need not sign your name, though you may if you wish. Many thanks for your help.

How would you rate this program overall? (circle one)

Excellent   Good   Fair   Poor

Did this program meet
- ❑ all of your expectations,
- ❑ most of your expectations,
- ❑ some of your expectations,
- ❑ none of your expectations?

In your opinion, did the program contain
- ❑ too much material for the time allotted,
- ❑ about the right amount of material,
- ❑ not enough material—too many sessions dragged?

How would you rate the administration of this program?
- ❑ Excellent—the program ran smoothly from start to finish.
- ❑ Good—most aspects of the program ran smoothly.
- ❑ Fair—only a few aspects of the program ran smoothly.
- ❑ Poor—no aspects of the program ran smoothly.

What have you learned from this program?

What should be done to improve this program in the future?

Please return this form to:

_____

_____

_____

Trainer Feedback Form

Following the format below, use the name of the actual exercises that were done or briefly identify each session. Make two separate evaluation sheets, one for the *session* and the other for the *facilitator*. (Include a set of responses for each session and each facilitator.)

Please rate the following individual sessions/facilitator: (check one)

Session/Facilitator	Excellent	Good	Fair	Poor

Please comment on those sessions you rated particularly high or low:

Variations on the Evaluation Process

Several more creative approaches to evaluation may challenge both the facilitator and the participants.

One approach is something like this:

> Before the workshop begins, the facilitator should handpick three participants who have the background, experience and maturity (but who do not necessarily have prior content knowledge of the subject) and give them the assignment of evaluating the workshop. They need be given no further instructions, other than to evaluate the facilitator(s), the exercises, and the workshop's attainment of the stated objectives. So long as they achieve these ends, they may do the job in any way they decide.

Several other nontraditional approaches are outlined in the March, 1980, issue of the *Bulletin on Training*.[22] These include:

1. Dividing the total workshop group into three equal teams and assigning each team the task of suggesting ways to improve one of the following aspects of the workshop: the course content, the methodology, or the logistical arrangements. Each of these small groups should then report orally to the whole group, while someone captures all the comments on a flip chart.

2. Dividing the group into pairs or triads and assigning each of these subgroups the task of coming up with two things that were especially memorable in the workshop or two suggestions for improving the workshop. These ideas should then be shared with the whole group while someone captures all the comments on a flip chart.

3. Forming a circle and having participants tell one thing they have learned from the course, allowing other members of the group to add comments as each point is made. These comments also should be captured on a flip chart. Ask participants what new perspectives they have gained as a result of the workshop. Have their attitudes changed, and if so, in what ways?

For further guidance on how to evaluate cross-cultural education and training programs see, "Evaluation: Some Practical Guidelines" by George Renwick. In *Multicultural Education: A Cross-Cultural Training Approach*, Margaret D. Pusch, ed. Yarmouth, ME: Intercultural Press, 1979.

Appendix A

Simulation Games

BaFá BaFá: A Cross-Cultural Simulation by R. Garry Shirts

This classic cross-cultural simulation game was developed in the early 1970s for the Navy. It has been used thousands of times since then in cross-cultural, multicultural, and diversity situations: Foreign Service families leaving on new overseas assignments, public school teachers endeavoring to improve communication with their multiethnic students, and government employees exploring issues of sex discrimination, to name only a few. Including its debriefing time, BaFá BaFá takes three hours or a little less and can be played by sixteen to forty (more if necessary) people. It is relatively nonthreatening and is an excellent stimulus for discussion of sensitive issues.

Participants are divided into two groups, sent to separate rooms, and given instructions on forming two very different cultures. After a short time of getting acclimated to their own cultures, participants, in groups of two or more, take turns visiting the "other" culture. In between visits, they discuss their observations with the people in their home culture. Once everyone has had a chance to visit, the game ends and an hour or so is spent discussing what happened in the simulation and the analogies which can be drawn to real-life, cross-cultural experiences. One of the most important issues highlighted by the simulation is the degree to which people bring misperceptions to the intercultural experience simply because they cannot observe others from any other viewpoint than that determined by their own cultural conditioning. Visitors frequently feel ill at ease, disoriented, and confused, just as one does in cross-cultural interaction—but much of this can be elicited from the postgame discussion when participants come to understand the cultural values and customs behind each other's external behavior.
Available from Simulation Training Systems, P.O. Box 910, Del Mar, CA 92014; (800) 942-2900.

Barnga: A Simulation Game on Culture Clashes by Sivasailam Thiagarajan and Barbara Steinwachs

This is the most flexible of simulations because it can be used with any number of players from nine to one hundred (or more) in a block of time ranging from one and a quarter to two and a half hours. It has been used with eighty college faculty members meeting statewide to enhance their campus cross-cultural studies programs, with thirty-five newcomers to the United States to explore adjusting to living in a new culture, and with ninety teenagers attending a conference on improving communication.

In the game, players form small groups and sit at a table together. Using written guidesheets, they learn a very simple card game and practice playing it. After a short time, the guidesheets are removed and a rule of "no oral communication" is imposed. They play on, silently. Then a tournament begins, and some from each table move up (or down) to other tables. Soon people are laughing, banging the tables, and gesturing wildly. What is going on? Unknown to the players (though some soon catch on), the guidesheets at each table are slightly different, and so is the card game. The misunderstandings, judgments, and biases which emerge from the slight differences are remarkable and serve to spark an energetic debriefing.

The game and its follow-up discussion are fun and stimulating. All participants do their best, but each group operates from a different set of circumstances and ground rules. Even when people discover the rules are different, they don't always know what the differences are or how to bridge them. The debriefing draws from the participants a wealth of related real-life experiences which greatly enhance the learning.

Available from Intercultural Press, P.O. Box 700, Yarmouth, ME 04096; (207) 846-5168.

Clues & Challenges: Culture-General Cross-Cultural Orientation by Sandra Mumford Fowler and Barbara Steinwachs with Pierre Corbeil, for Youth for Understanding

A "general orientation" cross-cultural simulation game. Works well with from as few as nine people to a very large group. Time: three hours (includes debriefing).

The game helps people understand the origins and meaning of "culture" and begin to recognize that people's actions, even when they appear strange, have roots in their own values, customs, and everyday experiences. It gives them the opportunity to practice making the transition from one culture to another.

In the game, participants form small groups, receive some clues (on cards), and try to solve the "mystery" of what kind of culture they might be a part of. Since the cards do not represent any real-world culture, the players actually build their cultures from scratch, using the clues as starters. They then face two challenges. In the first, they create an activity demonstrating something about their new culture. In the second, some from each culture get together to create an activity representing something important about all the new cultures. When the second challenge is completed, they discuss what happened, analyze what it meant, and apply the learning to real-world cross-cultural challenges. The game elicits sensitivity to different situations and creativity in dealing with them.

For information on availability, contact: Training Department, Youth for Understanding International Exchange, 3501 Newark Street, Washington, DC 20016.

Conducting Planning Exercises by Paul S. Twelker

Groups representing different interests generate proposed solutions to a problem. Facilitates the examination of alternative approaches to a given issue. This is a frame game that gives the facilitator a general format that can be adapted to a variety of specific situations. Since the format is flexible, this game can be played in a period of two to three hours or used in an ongoing class and played over several class periods. Printed directions.

Available from Simulation Systems, P.O. Box 1810, Sisters, OR 97759; (503) 595-6238.

Ecotonos by Nipporica Associates and Dianne Hofner Saphiere

Ecotonos is an excellent tool for engaging groups in problem solving and decision making. Methods and processes of decision making in monocultural and multicultural groups are analyzed, diagrammed, and compared. Generates guidelines for effectiveness when groups are composed of people from a variety of cultures. Participants enhance their understanding of the impact of culture on decision making and problem solving and develop their skills in participating effectively in a multicultural decision-making process. It is useful in domestic diversity as well as international contexts. It can be used several times with the same audience to assess progress or to deal with a variety of issues and is easily tailored to specific situations. From twelve to fifty people may participate.

Available from Intercultural Press, P.O. Box 700, Yarmouth, ME 04096; (207) 846-5168.

Markhall by James McCaffery, Daniel Edwards, Judee Blohm, and David Bachner

Markhall is an interactive and substantive simulation which explores the impact that different management styles have on the quality of life in the corporate workplace and on the products that come from it. It draws on corporate models existing in Japan and the U.S. Time: six to eight hours with debriefing. Directions and kit.

Available from Orientation and Language Series, Youth for Understanding, International Exchange, 3501 Newark St. NW, Washington, DC 20016; (202) 966-6808.

Starpower by R. Garry Shirts

This game, about the nature of power and how it affects those who have it and those who do not, takes from two and a half to three and a half hours, including debriefing. Directions and kit.

Available from Simulation Training Systems, P.O. Box 910, Del Mar, CA 92014; (800) 942-2900.

Synoptics by Susan Dearth and Leon McKenzie

This is a simple frame game which enables the players to view a problem situation from various perspectives. With debriefing time, it takes about two hours.

Send $1.00 to: Barbara Steinwachs, risingmoon, 1128 East Bluff Drive, Penn Yan, NY 14527; (315) 536-7895.

Talking Rocks by Robert Vernon

The origins of writing (cross-cultural communication across time) are explored. With debriefing time, this game takes between two and three hours. Booklet.

Available from Simulation Training Systems, P.O. Box 910, Del Mar, CA 92014; (800) 942-2900.

Where Do You Draw the Line? An Ethics Game by R. Garry Shirts

This simulation which focuses on what "should be" without excluding consideration of "what is," also works well as a frame game. The time to play and debrief this game is between one and three hours. Directions and kit.

Available from Simulation Training Systems, P.O. Box 910, Del Mar, CA 92014; (800) 942-2900.

Organizations/Publications

Organizations

ABSEL: Association for Business Simulation & Experiential Learning
Small professional association; holds annual conference; publishes comprehensive directory on business simulation games and their users. For information: J. Bernard Keys, Department of Management, Georgia Southern College, Statesboro, GA 30458; (912) 681-5457.

ISAGA: The International Simulation and Gaming Association
Small professional association; holds annual conference; most members from Europe. For information: Danny Saunders, Department of Behavioral and Communication Studies, The Polytechnic of Wales, Pontypridd, Mid Glamorgan, CF37 1DL, Wales (UK); (0443) 480480.

NASAGA: The North American Simulation and Gaming Association
Small professional association interested in advancing an optimal, responsible application of simulation games. Members receive subscription to *Simulation & Gaming.* Holds annual conference. NASAGA Executive Secretariat, John del Regato, Pentathalon Institute, P.O. Box 20590, Indianapolis, IN 46220; (317) 782-1553.

Publications

Callah, Madelyn R. (Ed.). *Get Results from Simulation and Role Play.* Alexandria, VA: American Society for Training and Development, 1985. INFO-LINE #412 (12/85).

Crookall, David, and Daniel Saunders (Eds.). *Communication and Simulation: From Two Fields to One Theme.* Philadelphia: Multilingual Matters, 1988.

Gillispie, Philip H. *Learning through Simulation Games.* New York: Paulist, 1973.

Greenbalt, Cathy S., and Richard D. Duke. *Principles and Practices of Gaming Simulation.* Thousand Oaks, CA: Sage, 1981.

Stolovitch, Harold D., and Sivasailam Thiagarajan. *Framegames.* Educational Technology Publications, 1980.

Thiagarajan, Sivasailam, and Harold D. Stolovitch. *Instructional Simulation Games.* Educational Technology Publications, 1978.

Simulation & Gaming: An International Journal of Theory, Design & Research. Thousand Oaks, CA: Sage. (NASAGA members receive subscription.)

Appendix B

Films and Videos

Sources

- *Crossing Cultures through Film* by Ellen Summerfield. Intercultural Press, P.O. Box 700, Yarmouth, ME 04096. (207) 846-5168. Analyzes and discusses over seventy classic films, with concrete suggestions for their use.
- *The Educational Film Locator* published by R. R. Bowker. Available in libraries. Useful for identifying films by subject, country and area.
- *Film and Video Resources for International Educational Exchange* by Lee Zeigler. NAFSA: Association of International Educators. Distributed by Intercultural Press, P.O. Box 700, Yarmouth, ME 04096. (207) 846-5168. A list of documentaries, feature films, audiovisuals and film distributors for those concerned with diversity, multiculturalism, and culture conflict.
- *Films for a Changing World: A Critical International Guide* by Jean Marie Ackerman. Society for International Development. Best source on classic, older cross-cultural films. (Out of print; available in libraries.)
- Pennsylvania State Audio-Visual Services, Special Services Building, University Park, PA 16802. Write for free film catalogues.
- Public Broadcasting Service. Check local PBS stations for films or series.
- University of California Extension Media Center, 2176 Shattuck Avenue, Berkeley, CA 94704. Write for free film catalogues.
- The Video Source Book published by Gale Research. Available in libraries. Useful for locating country-specific videos and films under the "Subject Category Index."

Selected Titles

- *The Ax Fight.* Deals with social conflict among the Yamomano Indians of Venezuela. 1975 (30 minutes). Available on 3/4" Umatic from Documentary Educational Resources, 5 Bridge Street, Watertown, MA 02172; (617) 926-0491.
- *The Ballad of Gregorio Cortez.* A commercial videotape starring Edward James Olmos of *Miami Vice* and *Stand and Deliver* fame. This is an historically based story of a Mexican farmer accused of killing a U.S. law officer as told from the perspectives of those who were involved. Excellent as a springboard for

discussions about stereotypes and differences in perception. 1982 (105 minutes). Available from your local video rental shop.

- *Bread and Chocolate.* Starring Nino Manfredi, this film portrays the trials and tribulations of an Italian waiter working in Switzerland. Humorous, with plenty of material for discussion. 1973 (111 minutes). Available on 16mm with subtitles from World Northal Corporation, 1 Dag Hammarskjöld Plaza, New York, NY 10017; (212) 223-8181. Also available in video stores.

- *Ceremony.* This sensitive Japanese film presents the eternal conflict between the old and the new in an engaging, provocative manner which is sure to elicit much self-examination and a great deal of stimulating discussion. 1971 (122 minutes). Available on 16mm from New Yorker Films, 16 West 61st Street, New York, NY 10023; (212) 247-6110.

- *Cold Water.* A video about culture shock and adaptation to American culture. An excellent documentary on how university-level foreign students view the U.S. and Americans. Focuses on reactions and adjustments to values and behaviors including such things as openness, directness, privacy, friendship, time management, mobility, competition, and self-reliance. Facilitator's handbook is included. 1987 (48 minutes). Available from Intercultural Press, P.O. Box 700, Yarmouth, ME 04096; (207) 846-5168.

- *Dances with Wolves.* One of the few commercial films to portray Native Americans in a positive manner as individuals albeit through a white man's eyes. It tells the story of Lieutenant John Dunbar's encounter with a band of Lakota Sioux in 1863 and his eventual acceptance into their way of life, including a new name, Dances with Wolves. Although probably too long (more than three hours) to show in its entirety, some scenes vividly illustrate the frustrations and humor involved in learning to adapt to a completely different culture. 1990 (190 minutes). Available from local video shops.

- *Dead Birds.* An ethnographic study of the Dani people of western New Guinea which will raise unanswerable questions for even the most intellectual audience. 1973 (83 minutes). Available on VHS from Phoenix Films & Video, 468 Park Avenue South, New York, NY 10012; (800) 221-1274, and CRM/McGraw-Hill Films, 674 Via de la Valle, P.O. Box 641, Del Mar, CA 92014; (619) 453-5000.

- *Doing Business in Japan: Negotiating a Contract.* Observes specific cultural differences in negotiations between Americans and Japanese. 1976 (35 minutes). Available on 16mm from Kent State University, Audiovisual Services, 330 Library Building, Kent, OH 44242; (216) 672-3456. Also available from University of Washington/Seattle, Instructional Media Services, 23 Kane Hall, DG-10, Seattle, WA 98195; (206) 543-9909.

- *El Norte*. Account of a Guatemalan brother and sister, persecuted in their homeland, who make the arduous journey north to the United States, where their dreams are barely realized. Heartrending and powerful. 1984 (141 minutes). Available in video stores.

- *Global Links*. A six-part series of 30-minute video programs developed by WETA-TV, Washington, DC and the World Bank to aid educators in teaching about Third World economic and social development. At the heart of the presentation is the "global link" or world interdependence that affects both the industrial and developing countries. The segments presented include "Traditions and the 20th Century," "Curse of the Tropics" (health and disease), "Women in the Third World," "Earth: The Changing Environment," "Education: A Chance for a Better World," and "The Urban Dilemma." Definitely worthwhile for those with little or no exposure to the Third World and our links with it. 1987. Available from WETA-TV, Educational Activities, P.O. Box 2626, Washington, DC 20013; (800) 445-1964.

- *The Gods Must Be Crazy*. What happens when a strange object (a Coke bottle) drops out of the sky into a Bushman's life? What problems does it cause his tribe and, later, him on his journey into Western society in an attempt to throw the bottle off the edge of the earth? Very funny movie with an intercultural theme. 1980 (109 minutes). Available in video stores.

- *Going International*. A series of seven films produced by Griggs Productions. Covers the subjects of culture, communication skills, adjusting to living and working abroad, reentry problems when returning home, and safety while living abroad. 1983. Available from Griggs Productions, 2046 Clement Street, San Francisco, CA 94121-2118; (415) 668-4200. Also available from Intercultural Press, P.O. Box 700, Yarmouth, ME 04096; (207) 846-5168.

- *The Japanese* Part I—*Full Moon Lunch*. This film follows a typical day in the Sugiyura family business. Aspects of Japanese culture are revealed through a depiction of methods of food preparation and family relationships. 1976 (58 minutes). Available from University of Illinois Film Center, 1325 South Oak Street, Champaign, IL 61820; (800) 367-3456.

- *Minorities in the Mainstream*. A series of videotaped vignettes, produced by the National Conference of Christians and Jews, which deals with the problems resulting from majority-minority working relationships. Available from National Conference of Christians and Jews, 71 Fifth Avenue, Suite 1100, New York, NY 10003; (212) 206-0006.

- *On Equal Terms: Sex Equity in the Workforce.* An examination of male and female roles in the United States and how these stereotypes are reinforced by culture. In this video we are made aware of how our gender helps shape our beliefs, careers, and relationships with each other. 1987 (30 minutes). Available from Barr Films, 12801 Schabarum Avenue, P.O. Box 7878, Irwindale, CA 91706-7878; (800) 234-7879.

- *Phantom India.* An impressionistic and humanistic interpretation of an exotic culture. 1972. This series of 16mm films is available from the University of Montana, Instructional Materials Service, Missoula, MT 59812; (406) 243-5976.

- *Valuing Diversity.* A series of three films produced by Griggs Productions which focuses on managing the multicultural work force, covering such subjects as stereotyping, cultural differences, communication styles, and problems which arise out of being bicultural. 1987. Available from Griggs Productions, 2046 Clement Street, San Francisco, CA 94121-2118; (415) 668-4200. Also available from Intercultural Press, P.O. Box 700, Yarmouth, ME 04096; (207) 846-5168.

- *Walkabout—Journey with the Aboriginals* (revised edition). A portrayal of life among the Aborigines in the Australian "outback." Sensitively made with striking cross-cultural insights. 1946 (17 minutes). Available on 16mm from University of Pittsburgh, Media Services, G-20 Hillman Library, Pittsburgh, PA 15260; (412) 624-4463.

- *Witness.* A popular, commercial videotape which presents a detective's dilemma when he discovers another policeman is involved in drugs. The detective ends up hiding in an Amish community, and the adaptation process both he and the Amish go through will provoke discussion. 1985 (112 minutes). Available in video stores.

- *The World of Apu.* The Satyjit Ray trilogy brings home the reality of India in a sympathetic, touching way. 1959 (103 minutes, subtitles). Available on video from Festival Films, 2841 Irving Avenue South, Minneapolis, MN 55408; (612) 870-4744. Also available from Hollywood Home Theatre, 1540 North Highland Avenue, Hollywood, CA 90028; (800) 621-0849 ext. 176 or Video Yesteryear, Box C, Sandy Hook, CT 06482; (800) 243-0987.

Appendix C

For Further Reading

- *American Ways—A Guide for Foreigners in the United States.* Gary Althen. Yarmouth, ME: Intercultural Press, 1988.
- *The Art of Crossing Cultures.* Craig Storti. Yarmouth, ME: Intercultural Press, 1989.
- *Beyond Experience: The Experiential Approach to Cross-Cultural Education* (2d ed.). Theodore Gochenour (Ed.). Yarmouth, ME: Intercultural Press, 1993.
- "Body Ritual among the Nacirema." Horace Miner. In Louise Fiber Luce and Elise Smith (Eds.), *Toward Internationalism: Readings in Cross-Cultural Communication* (2d ed.). Cambridge, MA: Newbury House, 1987.
- *Cows, Pigs, Wars, and Witches: The Riddles of Culture.* Marvin Harris. New York: Random House, 1989.
- *Crosscultural Understanding: Processes and Approaches for Foreign Language, English as a Second Language and Bilingual Educators.* Gail L. Nemetz Robinson. Elmsford, NY: Pergamon, 1985. (Out of print; available in libraries.)
- *The Cultural Dimension of International Business.* Gary P. Ferraro. Englewood Cliffs, NJ: Prentice-Hall, 1990.
- *Culture Learning: The Fifth Dimension in the Language Classroom.* Louise Damen. Reading, MA: Addison-Wesley, 1987.
- *Intercultural Communication: A Reader* (7th ed.). Larry A. Samovar and Richard E. Porter (Eds.). Belmont, CA: Wadsworth, 1994.
- *Intercultural Interactions: A Practical Guide.* Richard W. Brislin et al. Cross-Cultural Research and Methodology series, vol. 9 Thousand Oaks, CA: Sage, 1986.
- *Intercultural Sourcebook: Cross-Cultural Training Methodologies.* Sandra Mumford Fowler (Ed.). Yarmouth, ME: Intercultural Press, forthcoming.
- *An Introduction to Intercultural Communication.* John C. Condon and Fathi Yousef. New York: Macmillan, 1975.
- *Learning about Peoples and Cultures.* Seymour Fersh (Ed.). Evanston, IL: McDougal, Littell, 1989. (Out of print; available in libraries.)
- *Learning across Cultures* (2d ed.). Gary Althen (Ed.). Washington: NAFSA Association of International Educators, 1994.

- *Managing Cultural Differences* (2d ed.). Philip R. Harris and Robert T. Moran. Houston: Gulf, 1987.

- *Moving Abroad: A Guide to International Living.* Virginia McKay, 1990. Available from VLM Enterprises, P.O. Box 7236, Wilmington, DE 19803.

- "The Sacred Rac." Patricia Hughes. In Seymour Fersh (Ed.), *Learning about Peoples and Cultures.* Evanston, IL: McDougal, Littell, 1989. (Out of print; available in libraries.)

- *The Silent Language.* Edward T. Hall. New York: Doubleday, 1973. Also by E. T. Hall—*The Hidden Dimension* (1966), *Beyond Culture* (1976), and *The Dance of Life* (1983).

- *Survival Kit for Overseas Living* (2d ed.). L. Robert Kohls. Yarmouth, ME: Intercultural Press, 1984.

- *Toward Internationalism: Readings in Cross-Cultural Communication* (2d ed.). Louise Fiber Luce and Elise Smith (Eds.). Cambridge, MA: Newbury House, 1987.

- *Training for the Cross-Cultural Mind.* Pierre Casse. Washington: SIETAR International, 1980. Out of print; to be reissued in 1994 by Intercultural Press, Yarmouth, ME.

- *Understanding Intercultural Communication.* Larry Samovar, Richard E. Porter, and Nemi C. Jain. Belmont, CA: Wadsworth, 1981. (Out of print; available in libraries.)

Area Studies Resources

- *A Select Guide to Area Studies Resources.* L. Robert Kohls and V. Lynn Tyler. David M. Kennedy Center for International Studies, Brigham Young University, Provo, UT 84602, 1988. (Out of print; available in libraries.) One of the most complete bibliographies of all sources of area studies. See also *Guide to International Education in the United States.* David S. Hoopes and Kathleen R. Hoopes. Detroit: Gale Research, 1993. Lists resource information for 161 countries.

- "Background Notes" for 157 countries. Available from the Superintendent of Documents, U.S. Government Printing Office, Washington, DC 20402.

- Center for Area and Country Studies, Foreign Service Institute, U.S. Department of State, 1400 Key Boulevard, Arlington, VA 20520. Publishes excellent bibliographies for eight geographic regions of the world.

- Country Studies (formerly Area Handbooks). Foreign Area Studies Group at American University. Available from the Superintendent of Documents, U.S. Government Printing Office, Washington, DC 20402. Volumes available for 108 countries.

- *Updates* and *InterActs*. Intercultural Press, P.O. Box 700, Yarmouth, ME 04096. (207) 846-5168. Available for some fourteen countries.
- *Culturgrams*. David M. Kennedy Center for International Studies, Brigham Young University, Provo, UT 84602. Available for over 100 countries. Also, *Building Bridges of Understanding with the People of ___* for eleven countries. (Out of print; available in libraries.)
- Human Relations Area Files, 755 Prospect Street, New Haven, CT 06511. Provides access to voluminous entries of an anthropological nature on all the cultures and subcultures of the world. For the really serious student, copies of the file are also housed in major universities across the U.S.

Other Resources

- *Cross-Cultural Bibliography*. Virginia Foley and Janey Trowbridge. Overseas Briefing Center, Foreign Service Institute, U.S. Department of State, 1400 Key Boulevard, Arlington VA, 20520; 1990. The best general bibliography.
- *Intercultural Communicator Resources*. H. Ned Seelye and V. Lynn Tyler. Language and Intercultural Research Center of Brigham Young University, Provo, UT 84602, 1977. (Out of print; available on ERIC microfiche).
- SIETAR International. (International Society for Intercultural Education, Training and Research), 808 17th Street, NW, Suite 200, Washington, DC 20006. Professional association.
- Intercultural Communication Institute, 8835 S.W. Canyon Lane, Suite 238, Portland, OR 97225. Training center for intercultural specialists.
- *Cultural Diversity at Work*, published monthly by GilDeane Group, 13751 Lake City Way NE, Suite 105, Seattle, WA 98125. Good source for newer publications and culture-general and specific resources.

Endnotes

1. For more icebreaking activities see Sue Forbess-Greene, *The Encyclopedia of Icebreakers: Structured Activities That Warm Up, Motivate, Challenge, Acquaint, & Energize.* University Associates, 8517 Production Avenue, San Diego, CA 92121.

2. The Form is from *Culture Learning: The Fifth Dimension in the Language Classroom* by Louise Damen. Reading, MA: Addison-Wesley, 1987.

3. For more information on the Kluckhohn Model and how values fit into it see Appendix A in L. Robert Kohls, *Survival Kit for Overseas Living* (2d ed.). Yarmouth, ME: Intercultural Press, 1984.

4. Concept of Value Option Cards invented by Mobley, Luciani & Associates, 16 West 16th Street, New York, NY 10011.

5. As reported in David S. Hoopes and Paul Ventura (Eds.), *Intercultural Sourcebook: Cross-Cultural Training Methodologies.* Intercultural Press, Yarmouth, ME: 1979 (out of print.) A more complete description of Kraemer's work may be found in *Development of a Cultural Self-Awareness Approach to Instruction in Intercultural Communication* (Technical Report 73-17; HumRRO, Alexandria, VA, 1973.)

6. Francis L. K. Hsu. *The Study of Literate Civilizations.* New York: Holt, Rinehart & Winston, 1969.

7. Philip R. Harris and Robert T. Moran. *Managing Cultural Differences* (2d ed.). Table 4-1, "U.S. Values and Possible Alternatives." Houston: Gulf, (1987): 76-7.

8. John P. Fieg and John G. Blair. *There Is a Difference: Seventeen Intercultural Perspectives.* Washington: Meridian House International, 1975.

9. Anthony Scarangello (Ed.). *American Education through Foreign Eyes.* New York: Hobbs, Dorman, 1967.

10. Griggs Productions, 2046 Clement Street, San Francisco, CA 94121-2118. (415) 668-4200.

11. George W. Renwick. Revised by Reginald Smart and Don L. Henderson. *A Fair Go for All: Australian/American Interactions.* Yarmouth, ME: Intercultural Press, (1991): 22-4.

12. For more information on the subject of stereotyping as an "initial guide to reality," see Nancy Adler, *International Dimensions of Organizational Behavior.* Boston: Kent, (1986): 57-60.

13. This is intended to be provocative.

14. Additional information and exercises can be found in Pierre Casse, *Training for the Cross-Cultural Mind*. Washington: SIETAR International, 1980 (out of print; to be reissued in 1994 by Intercultural Press, Yarmouth, ME).

15. For information on perception see one of the following: *Illusion in Nature and Art*. R. L. Gregory and E. M. Gombrich (Eds.). London: Duckworth, 1973 or *Readings from Scientific American: Recent Progress in Perception*, with introductions by Richard Held and Whitman Richards. San Francisco: W. H. Freeman, 1976.

16. Theodore Gochenour (Ed.). *Beyond Experience: The Experiential Approach to Cross-Cultural Education* (2d ed.). Intercultural Press, Yarmouth, ME: (1993): 143-7.

17. See Louise Fiber Luce and Elise Smith (Eds.). *Toward Internationalism: Readings in Cross Cultural Communication* (2d ed.). Cambridge: Newbury House, 1987. See pp. 27-9 for Horace Miner's "Body Ritual among the Nacirema."

18. Paul Pedersen called this exercise the "Culture Shock Game." Under that name the exercise was demonstrated at the 1981 SIETAR Conference in Vancouver, British Columbia, Canada.

19. The introduction to the case studies has been adapted from V. Lynn Tyler's draft of *People to People: A Synergic Intercultural Casebook*. Features samples from the many publications of the Brigham Young University David M. Kennedy Center for International Studies, 280 HRCB, Provo, UT 84602.

20. The Peace Corps Library at 1990 K Street, NW, Washington, DC. Not intended to serve the general public, but has endless resources from its many training programs, and it has been most generous in sharing its riches. See Endnote 19 for the address of the David M. Kennedy Center for International Studies.

21. By Robert J. Foster and David T. O'Nan. Human Resources Research Organization, 300 North Washington Street, Alexandria, VA 22314, 1967.

22. Published by BNA Communication, Inc., Rockville, MD 20850.

About the Authors

L. Robert Kohls is Senior Research Fellow at the San Francisco-based management consulting firm of Global Vision Group. Retired in 1993 from the position of Director of the Office of International Programs at San Francisco State University, he has thirty years' experience as an intercultural trainer and trainer of other trainers. With over 120,000 copies in print, his *Survival Kit for Overseas Living* is considered a classic in the field. Kohls has lived, worked, and traveled in more than eighty countries with extensive stays in Asia, Africa, the Middle East and Latin America. A founding member of SIETAR International, he was, in 1986, the first recipient of the Society's most prestigious award, Primus inter pares.

John M. Knight is a professor at Saint Mary's College of California in Moraga. He began his cross-cultural experiences as an Air Force "brat" in Germany in the 1950s and continued them with four years as a Peace Corps volunteer in Ethiopia. Afterward, he worked with the Papago Indians in Tucson, Arizona, while pursuing his master's degree. He then spent six years teaching English in Saudi Arabia. Since returning to the States, in addition to teaching he has conducted cross-cultural communication programs for Pacific Gas & Electric, Stauffer Chemical Company, Heublein Wines, Mitsubishi Bank, and Glendale Adventist Medical Center.